100% CHOICE

Becoming
a conscious
creator of
your life

Sharon Shahaf

Sharon Shahaf

100% CHOICE

Becoming a Conscious Creator of Your Life

....

Copyright © 2020 Sharon Shahaf

All rights reserved. No part of this book may be reproduced in any form or by any electronic or mechanical means, including information storage and retrieval systems, without permission in writing from the author, except by reviewers, who may quote brief passages in a review.

Cover design: Ilanit Cohen Fridman

Front cover image: Imagebank / Getty Images

ISBN: 978-9659282722 (Paperback)

Contact: info@sharonshahaf.com

Dedicated to my mother, without whom my journey wouldn't have been possible.

Contents

Preface 9
The Five Wondrous Powers 9
Introduction 12
Current Situation 13
Transforming Reality 14

PART ONE—*Who Is Creating Your Reality?*

Who Is Creating Your Reality? 16
Chapter 1—Parents and Children—The Saga of Human Pain 17
"I'm Not Good Enough!" 18
How Your Family Can Create Your Biggest Pain 20
From Freedom to Slavery—Parenting in the Modern Age ...29
Destructive Defense Mechanisms 31
Breaking the Circle of Pain 36
Chapter 2—A Culture of Fear and Lack of Control. 45
The Rule of Fear 45
The Lack of Control Deception 49
Chapter 3—Who Is Running the Show of Your Life? 58
Over-Sensitivity 58
Raging Emotional Pain 60
Running Away from Your Feelings of Worthlessness 61

PART TWO — *Awakening*

Chapter 4 — Awaken from the Bad Dream 66
What Is Awakening? 66
Are You Already Awakening? 67
The Three Foundations of Awakened Life 68
Simple Yet Profound Change 71

Chapter 5 — Being: The Magical Dimension of Life 73
The Failure of Modern-Age Thought Patterns 73
The Ticket to Your New Life: Meet Presence 79
Meditation Won't Help If You Don't Understand This 84
Presence as a Problem Solver 88
The Joy of Being 92

PART THREE — *Consciousness, Responsibility, and Choice*

Chapter 6 — Emotions: The Key to Success 96
Why Are Your Emotions Making You Miserable? 97
Acknowledging the Underlying Emotion to Heal the Pain .. 108
Is Your Anger Normal? 114
How Can You Control Your Emotions? 121
The Mysterious Switch That Will Help You Give Up Your Negativity 131
Negativity's Battle for Survival 132
Effortless Self-Love 133
From Fear to Love 134
Love 139
One Energy — How Everything Is Connected 142
Emotions as an Inner Guide 145

Chapter 7 — Conscious Creation 147
Full Responsibility — Getting Control Back into Your Hands 148
The Influence of Your Inner Energy on the Reality of Your Life 154

What Do You Really Want? 161
Conscious Choices and Sensible Decision-Making 170
The Foundation of Self-Acceptance 175
The World as a Giant Mirror That Reflects What's Inside Us 182
Becoming Free of the Need for Control 190
Impeccability 196

PART FOUR—*Creation and Fulfillment*

Chapter 8—Changing from the Outside In 200
Laying the Groundwork for Change 200
Why Are People Treating Me This Way? 202
How Do Words Create Reality? 203
The Simplest Way to Get the Attitude You Wish For 215
Supporting the Process of Change 221

Chapter 9—Reality Creation 223
Preparing for Success 223
Manifestation 235

Afterword 245
The Principles Presented in This Book 245
It Is All a Choice 247
A Glimpse into the Future 247
Conclusion 248

A Guide to Practicing Presence 249
References 263

Preface

The Five Wondrous Powers

When God created the Earth he gave his creations—mankind—five wondrous powers through which they could lead fulfilling and prosperous lives. "These powers will always be with you," he said. "They are the key to all you'll ever need."

The power of thought was given to humans to be used as a compass. To encourage creativity, God did not give humans control over their thoughts; he did, however, give them the ability to observe their minds. "Thoughts will evoke emotions, which, in turn, will remind you to examine your thoughts. Eventually, your thoughts will become a physical reality that reflects the content of your minds. And when you get tired of the game of thought, you can always reunite with me and rest without thought."

Over time, the initial intention of the power of thought was forgotten. Humans forgot how to observe their minds to learn about the reality shaped by their thoughts, as well as how to take a break from thinking. They mixed up the order of things and came to believe it was the circumstances that created their painful thoughts, failing to remember it was their thoughts that created the unwanted circumstances.

The power of observation was given to humans so they would be able to understand the world, the animals, and the people around them. "Look around," God said. "Listen carefully," he added, "not to the words, as they will deceive you, but to what's behind them, to what's not being said: to a tone of voice, to a gap between the words, to a sigh, and to pain reflected through the eyes; to a dog's wagging tail or to its raised hackles."

But the initial intention of the power of observation was soon forgotten. Instead of listening to the world, humans started listening to the words—the words that were used to hide true feelings, the words that covered the truth. They no longer believed they could simply look and listen in order to know what's going on. Confused, they keep trying to find answers in the chaos of their minds or in words that seldom reveal more than they hide.

The power of will was given to humans so they would be able to create anything they wanted. "Wish for something, get excited about it, visualize it as if it was real, and it will be yours," God said.

And though humans wanted many things, they didn't feel excited about them; instead, they were filled with fear. "What if I won't achieve what I want? What if I miss the chance?" fear whispered in their minds. And what filled their minds manifested in their lives.

The power of play was given to humans so they would be able to play with creation, gain experiences, have fun, and learn. "Be passionate and creative, and play as if everything is possible," God said. "Aim to achieve your true desires, and if you fail, simply learn from it and create another game."

Once again, humans forgot the initial intention of the exceptional gift they received. They started taking life too seriously and were reluctant to use their creativity, fearing someone would judge their creation as not good enough. Eventually, they stopped trying at all. "What if I fail again?" they asked.

The power of love, which includes the rest of the powers within it, was given to humans by God as a symbol of his love for them. God wanted humans to feel as joyous as he felt when he created them and to always remember who they truly are. "This power," he said, smiling, "will bring abundance, happiness, and blessing into your lives and provide you with the ability to fulfill all your dreams."

Not surprisingly, humans have forgotten how to use this power too. They mixed up real love with being in love, the short-lived thrill that may easily turn into emotional dependency, and instead of acting out of love, fear controlled everything they did.

When the five wondrous powers were forgotten, the world became a grayish and intimidating place. Everything felt difficult, and people's lives were filled with problems they believed they must solve in order to start "truly living." "God doesn't exist," they bitterly claimed, "if he did exist, he wouldn't have let all of this happen: The Holocaust, hungry children, pain, fear, and illness." "If God existed," they added, "he would have already given me what I want so much."

And God looked at his beloved children from above with a heart full of pain. He tried to send them messages in every possible way to show them how they could change their lives. But they wouldn't listen or distorted his messages, and kept using the exact same methods that never led them where they aimed.

Many years went by, years of great achievements and development, as well as huge destruction, wars, and pain.

Today, after tediously running from one expert to another, trying to improve things in customary ways, many have begun to suspect that something is fundamentally wrong and that maybe all that has been said so far is not the answer to the puzzle of their lives. And as the pain intensifies, so does the urge to regain access to the five wondrous powers that have always been with them.

∴

"The five wondrous powers" is a tale, as well as the deepest truth of who you really are and who you are meant to be, no matter what your current circumstances are.

Introduction

Ten years ago, while looking for relief from emotional pain, I consulted a palm reader. At the end of her analysis she concluded, "Change is a long process. Even if you work hard and spend years achieving it, you shouldn't expect too much."

I was angry. Though her words reflected the fundamental beliefs of the medical establishment, and though at the time "ease" was a foreign term in my life, there was a clear knowing within me that what I was looking for existed: a simple yet profound change that would transform me into someone I had vaguely known, yet, in a way, had always missed.

Seven years have passed since this meeting, during which my journey continued. I tried different healing methods and experienced success as well as failure and disappointment, until finally I found what I was always looking for and got to meet the one I always longed for—myself! Who I truly am.

Current Situation

Difficulty finding a life partner or maintaining a fulfilling relationship, massive confusion around the right way to parent, a never-ending battle against weight gain, constant feelings of frustration, stress, emptiness, or depression. Running from therapists to mystics or hanging on to gurus' words, wishing for answers or at least for a moment of relief.

In the news—wars, political power struggles, continual violence, and horrors.

Numerous children are being diagnosed with Attention-Deficit/Hyperactivity Disorder (ADHD), or with Autism Spectrum Disorder (ASD). Young children are suffering from stress, anxiety, or obesity. Increasing numbers of people are struggling with chronic or fatal diseases, eating disorders, or addictions, or they "only" experience deep dissatisfaction with themselves and their lives.

Endless contradicting theories tell us how we should behave, what we should think, feel, want, or eat. Every now and again a new method promises to be "the one" that will bring salvation to mankind. It seems that handling modern life has become too complicated and the full operating guide is nowhere to be found.

You might be thinking that you are the only one who feels this way; that only your thoughts are driving you crazy, that you are the only one who cannot enjoy life, that something is fundamentally wrong with you.

However, the situations described above are merely a reflection of what's currently going on within all of us; hardly anyone these days feels really happy or even content. Yet, as it's a social norm to maintain a positive image above all, nearly everyone covers the truth with prettification and denial.

Transforming Reality

So how can we transform our reality, both on a personal and on a collective level? The answer is simple; it is based on only two principles:

1. You are creating your own reality.
2. The moment of power is always the now.

This is the entire story.

This truth has been told many times and in various ways, but it has often been ignored, misunderstood, or twisted.

In a clear and practical way, that cannot be misinterpreted, I will present you with the answer and show you how you can implement these two principles to create a fulfilling and satisfying life.

PART ONE

Who Is Creating Your Reality?

Who Is Creating Your Reality?

Our beliefs, thoughts, and emotions are the raw materials of our lives. When we want something and believe it is possible, it will manifest in our lives. When we believe it's complicated and unachievable, this is what we experience.

Our thoughts shape the way our reality looks and determine the way we feel. Most of us, however, are hardly aware of the content of our minds.

If you listen to your thoughts, you will find that instead of focusing on your goals, your attention is often drawn to the fear that you won't achieve them, to dissatisfaction with *what is* and what you haven't achieved so far, and to regrets about the past. You will find that your mind is constantly busy with other people's stuff, with power struggles, with resentments, grudges, revenge planning, or self-criticism. You will find that you are constantly running away from thinking, as you fear what comes up in the quiet moments you couldn't avoid.

Some new-age teachings claim that we have full control over our thoughts and emotions; that we can choose not to feel offended, not to get angry, control the content of our minds, and love ourselves by a simple choice. Could that be true? Such assumptions, although pointing to the truth, are misleading. The assumption that controlling thoughts and emotions is a matter of a rational decision that anyone can make is wrong. If you are honest with yourself, you have to admit that no matter how hard you try to "think positively" and convince yourself that you have no reason to feel what you are feeling, unwanted thoughts and emotions find their way back into your mind.

By pointing this out I have no intention to put an end to your hopes for a better life. On the contrary, in the following chapters I'm going to show you the reasons that stand in your way of becoming the master of your life, and to explain what you can do to regain control.

Chapter 1

Parents and Children
The Saga of Human Pain

It is not a coincidence that I'm opening this book with the story of human pain, the story about parents and children, about the pain that passes from one generation to another. My clients hardly ever come to me in order to resolve conflicts with their parents. They come to find what stands between them and the relationship they desire, to discover their purpose in life, to achieve weight loss, to improve self-confidence, or to break free from the emotional and behavioral patterns that stand in their way toward their goals. Some of them have already been to therapy and gained some understanding about their relationships with their parents; others are afraid to look into this place or consider it a waste of time.

The belief, however, that circumstances can make us happy is only a myth. Without dealing with the root cause of our issues, no matter what we achieve, the same thought patterns, accompanied by dissatisfaction and pain, will haunt us.

Our current issues are always rooted in our childhood. As children, we were influenced by our relationships with our parents, by their relationship as a couple, by our position in the family, and most strongly, by the mental and emotional health of our parents during our childhood.

Yet, our issues and pain are not a direct outcome of what we have suffered. They are rooted in our past experiences but kept alive in the present moment by deep-seated thinking, behavioral, and emotional patterns. When we are free of those, the main part of the challenges we face magically disappears, and the path toward our goals opens.

So let's have a look at how it all began and how we can set ourselves free from the pain.

"I'm Not Good Enough!"

The feeling of not being "enough" (beautiful, smart, or successful), which seems to most people a unique and personal problem, is deeply entrenched in our culture.* Few are those who are free of it, although the masks that are customarily worn in our society make you think that you are the only one who feels this way, except, maybe, for some unfortunate others who are not comparable to you anyway.

Where does this feeling of lack come from? Every human, like every living being, is born with a sense of wholeness. But since the way we learn to know ourselves is through the feedback provided by those around us, infants learn to know themselves through the way their parents treat them. In nature things are clear—as long as required, the mother will

---

* The terms "our culture," "our society," and "cultural," which appear throughout the book, refer to contemporary society as a whole.

devote herself to her offspring. She will feed them, protect them, guide them lovingly, and in due course, release them to live their lives on their own. In the ordinary course of nature, the role of any parent is to provide his or her offspring with a sense of security and with the knowledge that will enable them to cope effectively with life. The human-animal is no different—human beings have the same instinct to love their children, to care for them with devotion, to guide them by example, and, as they mature, to let them live their lives according to their wishes. However, few are the parents who are capable of providing this kind of love to their children.

The kind of love I am talking about—unconditional love—is the ability to fully answer the child's emotional needs, without expecting anything in return, and regardless of external appearance, gender, personal characteristics, or achievements.

A child who doesn't enjoy such love learns to doubt his self-worth and develops a burning desire to fill the void he feels within, accompanied by the fear that the void will never be filled and that the pain will never ease. Another feeling that develops around the absence of unconditional love is anger. Anger comes from the inner knowing that exists in every human being, even if he is not aware of it and cannot put it in words, that by nature he is worthy, complete, and whole. The anger is directed toward those who the child instinctively feels were supposed to acknowledge his (or her) inherent worth and failed.

As a consequence, self-doubt, emotional pain, anger, and fear are feelings that each one of us carries on some level.

Why, then, do so many parents fail to provide their children with unconditional love? Simply because they are still looking for it themselves. People cannot give credence to the worth of others as long as they don't recognize their own worth. They cannot answer the emotional needs of others when they are still occupied with their own emotional needs. They cannot be attentive to others when they are overwhelmed by frustration and pain. And they cannot grant unconditional love when, in their own eyes, they have not yet fulfilled the conditions that make them worthy of such love.

You may get furious reading these words and think, "They can; they just don't want to. It's not important enough to them!" "They shouldn't have had children if they can't!" or, "Why should I care about their troubles?"

How Your Family Can Create Your Biggest Pain

The feeling that my family is different and that everyone else's situation is better is something I well remember from my childhood. I used to think that the way I felt was a result of my personal circumstances and therefore unique to me. But to my surprise, over the years I have discovered that many people feel the same about their families.

Although on the surface there is a significant difference in the circumstances of different families, there is no direct relationship between the external circumstances and the inner experience of the child within the family, and even when everything seems perfect, a child may experience enormous pain. Many will find this notion difficult to grasp, since we all tend to interpret things from our own perspective. Thus, when someone has something we long for, we automatically assume that his or her situation is better than ours, without being able to understand his or her feelings or accept them as legitimate. In practice, what determines the child's experience in the family unit is the mental and emotional health of the parents, and accordingly their ability to meet his or her needs.

In order to achieve a significant and lasting transformation, we must first gain a clear understanding of the current situation. Therefore, I will begin by presenting the basic principles that create and sustain the emotional pain that passes from one generation to another.

The Impact of Your Inner Energy on Your Child's Well-Being

Even before we examine the impact of the family members' attitudes toward the child on him or her, we have to take into account the emotional energy that filled the home environment as a consequence of the mental and emotional health of the parents.

We all intuitively feel emotional energies. We know when someone is sad or angry even if he or she says that everything is okay, sometimes we instantly dislike a certain person without being able to understand why we feel this way, and when someone develops an unwanted dependency on us we automatically feel a sense of suffocation. Young children, because they are so open and receptive, are strongly influenced by emotional energy and are, therefore, deeply affected by their parents' inner state.

The child will be influenced by the true feelings of the parents regardless of what is revealed on the surface. If the parent is frightened of what is about to happen yet declares, "Everything will be all right," the child intuitively feels that something is wrong.

No child has ever gained self-confidence through a rational

explanation of how to be confident or through statements such as, "Don't be like me." Children learn through energetic influence (they experience the confidence that their parents feel) and through personal example (they see their parents behaving confidently).

Before experiencing a shift in my life, I was extremely frustrated with myself when I reacted to different situations just like my mother. I was offended and angry in the same situations she was, the social struggles I experienced as an adolescent were almost identical to what she experienced, and the way people reacted toward us was similar. I believed I'd inherited these character traits and that apart from trying to "overcome myself," nothing could be done to change it. Today I understand that these were emotional patterns that I absorbed from her, both through direct exposure to her reactions and through energetic exposure to her emotional energy.

Often a daughter of a mother who struggled with an eating disorder finds herself dealing with this issue as well. A child who suffers from anxiety discovers that his father also suffered from it. And a woman who is repeatedly caught in hopeless relationships finds out that her mother, before marrying her father, was involved with a man who had not chosen her as his partner. In such situations, the destructive pattern passes as an "energetic inheritance" of pain, sometimes even without the child being aware of what the parent has experienced.

Although their condition may not necessarily replicate that of their parents, the inner state of parents—fears, emotional burdens, and self-esteem—inevitably affects children, as if the emotional energy of their parents was a kind of marinade, immersing the children day after day.

I have come to understand that the mental and emotional health of the parents, especially that of the parent more significant to the child, affects the child more than anything else he or she experiences throughout life.

"This Kid Is Driving Me Crazy!"

Though most parents react differently to each of their children, they are often reluctant to admit that they favor one child over another. In such situations, even if the parent makes an effort to compensate the less favored child, the child can still sense what's going on beneath the surface, and most children express their frustration about it. To be precise, I would say that it's not necessarily greater love that the parent feels toward one child but greater acceptance; the preferred child easily evokes affection in the parent and therefore the parent tends to be more lenient with him or her, while the less favored child evokes irritation no matter what he or she does.

Sometimes the child is a living reminder of the weaknesses the parent has not yet overcome. In other cases, the child, in appearance or behavior, reminds the parent of a spouse he or she resents. Arbitrary aspects such as gender, appearance, interests, or skills may also affect the level of acceptance of the child.

When our parents don't accept us as we are, anger arises and self-doubt develops.

Whose Feelings Are These?

Many parents find it difficult to face their children's emotions without projecting on the situation the thought of what they would have felt in their place. This may happen when the child faces challenges similar to those the parent has faced in the past, such as being bullied or overweight. In other cases, the parent projects his or her own pain onto the child's situation while creating an imaginary drama in which the child is in pain. For example, a mother who finds it difficult to accept her own mother's death tells herself that her children could have been much happier if their grandmother was alive. In practice, although the children might have benefited from the relationship with their grandmother, they are much more affected by the sense of loss that their mother cultivates than by the absence of their grandmother from their lives.

When facing a challenge, what a child needs more than anything is the confidence and faith that he can cope with the situation; being treated as strong and capable by his parents enables the child to develop this sense of confidence. When the parents, instead, project their emotional pain onto the situation and overprotects the child, the child learns to believe that he is weak and incapable of coping on his (or her) own.

As a child, I was jealous of my twin sister when people said she was prettier than me. When I shared my feelings with my mother, she tried to prove to me that I'm not less than my sister and that there are areas in which I am stronger than her. Her words, however, did not make me feel better; on the contrary, her attempts to protect me made me feel weak. And although it was never said, I felt she was sorry for me—as being considered less pretty than her sister was a painful childhood experience of hers.

To be able to not feel sorry for their children and to see them as strong and capable, parents must first stop feeling sorry for themselves and see themselves as strong and capable.

"Eventually It's Always About Him"

Most adults are still looking for the sense of unconditional love they lacked in childhood. Once they have rationally understood that they probably won't get it from their parents, they turn to seek it in romantic relationships. But the attempt to fill the lack of unconditional love this way is destined to end in failure, for in a healthy and reciprocal relationship between two adults one cannot be responsible for the emotional wellbeing of the other. When their partner fails to fill the void, many turn to what seems to be the ideal solution—their children—and say to themselves, "I will have a child and he will really love me."

When a parent carries such an expectation, even if unconsciously, he or she can easily become angry and disappointed should he or she feel that the child doesn't love him or her enough. And through the painful place within him- or herself, the parent might easily interpret the child's actions as a sign of insufficient love.

Often when a conflict occurs between a parent and a child, and what the child needs is an adult's guidance on how to cope with his or her feelings, the parent's old pain arises and with it the expectation that the child will understand and support him or her. And the child wonders in frustration, "How did he/she become the center of the attention again?"

Is There Such a Thing as Too Much Love?

Many people get jealous when they see the affection that others receive from their parents. But sometimes behind such an enviable display of love hides a parent who loves his or her children too much. Unlike unconditional love, which carries no need or expectation, excessive love is driven by the parent's need to provide him- or herself with a sense of purpose through the relationship and satisfy his or her emotional needs.

Since such love involves a strong motive of emotional dependency, the parent may have an unrealistic need for the child to always be happy, as his or her own happiness depends on it. When the parent says, "I can't sleep at night worrying about you," he or she believes that such a statement demonstrates good and caring parenting. The parent overlooks the fact that the burden of his or her feelings adds to what the child is already coping with, and instead of providing support, the reaction might encourage the child to keep his or her true feelings hidden in the future, in order not to upset the parent.

Because the role of "the strong parent" is the parent's source of power, he or she may find it hard to give the child freedom and treat him or her as an adult, even when the child is already grown up.

"At Least I'm Not like My Mother!"

Many parents are not sure what kind of parents they want to be, but they are crystal clear about what kind of parents they don't want to be—similar to their parents. The primary goal of such parents is to prove that they are better than their parents.

A mother who grew up feeling that her mother favored her brother may deliberately focus on making her children feel equally loved. However, since she is driven by the need to be better than her mother, there might be something rigid and even forceful in her attempts. Determined to create equality, she might miss the chance to encourage the uniqueness of each child, or she may feel intimidated when one child's achievements surpass the other's and find herself discouraging the more successful child. She might be blind to the impact of her actions—to the direct pain she is causing one child and the indirect pain caused to the other, the one she is trying to protect, who learns to perceive him- or herself as weak, as someone who needs constant protection. Her goal is to make the weaker child more confident, yet the message of her actions is that achieving a sense of confidence requires putting others down, hurting them, and restricting their advancement.

A father who was treated with a firm hand by his parents may find it hard to set the necessary boundaries for his children, fearing to be "bad" like his parents. He may avoid discipline even when it's needed and neglect his own needs in favor of his children's desires.

Sometimes parents cause their children pain similar to the pain they suffered from their parents, yet as long as things look better on the surface, they can still say to themselves, "At least I'm not like my parents."

Emotional Manipulations

Conditional love is the outcome of unconditional love's absence. It involves emotional blackmail and manipulations that aim to force the child to act in the way the parent thinks is right. The weapon is the parent's love and affection. Emotional manipulations are often justified by wanting what's best for the child, while hiding a compulsive need for control.

Common manipulations are demonstrating

disappointment and anger, using threats, blaming, and crying. Such manipulations create a huge emotional burden on small children as well as on grown-ups and force them to look for immediate relief, which causes them to beg, bend, overlook their wishes, and restrict their own freedom.

By using manipulations parents often achieve their goals and enjoy short-term satisfaction, but the negative impact of such tactics is far-reaching; apart from affecting the relationship, by using emotional manipulations parents send a repeated message to their children that their choices are never good enough—that is to say, that they are never good enough.

Numerous adults keep fighting their parents' manipulations for years or align with them while conquering immense resentment. Guilt, as well as fear of the possible outcome the parent uses as a threat, makes it hard to simply say, "I understand it's only a manipulation, so I will ignore it."

Disrespect, Violence, and Abuse

As most grown-ups (and therefore most parents) carry heavy emotional burdens, even the most loving parents might be tempted to enjoy a moment of relief. Seeking to turn their frustration somewhere, the child becomes an easy target.

These harmful emotional outlets might include disrespectful behavior toward the child, using aggressive or derogatory intonation, casting arbitrary rules without reasonable explanation, or using disproportionate punishments. At the far end of the scale, there is physical, verbal, and emotional abuse.

The child, who cannot understand that the parent is not responding directly to his or her actions but rather to his own frustration, perceives him- or herself as guilty and his or her behavior as terrible.

From time to time, when the parent is having a moment of clarity and understands the consequences of his actions, he hurries to admit he (or she) was wrong and ask for forgiveness. But after a while the child understands that regardless of the pretty words, the offensive behavior will soon return. Thus, the apology provides no relief; on the contrary, it forces the child to repress his or her anger and frustration, as it seems wrong not to forgive someone who asked so nicely for forgiveness.

A child who is treated with disrespect feels small and humiliated, and often turns into an adult who needs to humiliate others to ease his or her feelings of inferiority.

From Freedom to Slavery—Parenting in the Modern Age

Modern-day parenting is somewhat opposite to what nature determined—in many ways it's the children who dictate the household's agenda. Often the loss of parental authority is so radical that the children can easily force their way. A mother who told me how her daughter persuades her to sit by her bed for a long time every night described her feeling as being raped. When she heard the words coming out of her mouth she panicked and swiftly justified her surrender by saying, "If it's so important to her, why wouldn't I make the extra effort?" At that moment she overlooked the relationship between constantly giving in to her children's demands and her impatience, rage outbursts, and exhaustion. Eventually, feeling guilty about her reactions was what drove her to give in once again.

Loss of inner authority is the main reason for the helplessness many parents experience. While in nature every creature is guided by its instincts to treat itself and its offspring wisely, with the development of modern life the human animal is losing touch with its inherent knowledge, and as a result the need for external guidance increases. That is the setting for the unimaginable number of life advisors who guide us on how to act in any aspect of our lives, including, of course, as parents. Unfortunately, the more we lean on external guidance, the less we trust the knowledge within us. Most often, it's not that parents don't know what to do, it's that they do not dare to listen to themselves and trust their own judgment.

Parents' permissiveness makes children realize they can get anything they want as long as they are stubborn enough; when the parent declares "one last piece of chocolate" and then gives in to the child's pressure, the child learns that the parent doesn't honor his or her word, and thus doesn't honor him- or herself. The parents' actions provide the child with a legitimate reason to treat the parent disrespectfully, just as the parent treats him- or herself.

Children may feel satisfaction at achieving their objectives, but in the long term the over-flexible boundaries do not serve them. It doesn't take long until they become enormously frustrated when they discover that the outside world is not all about them. The child who understands, even if unconsciously, that the parent is afraid of his or her reactions (thus, of him or her) feels victory for a moment, yet with this understanding comes fear and an unspoken question: "If my parents are afraid of me, how can they help me in dealing with my fears?" That's why, unconsciously, kids keep pushing their parents to the corner, desperately hoping to find someone to lean on.

There are many kinds of treatments available to solve the varied problems of today's children. But since the child's condition is merely a reflection of the parents' condition, treating the child or even the child and the parent together won't be enough. The solution should start where the problem has begun: in the mental and emotional state of the parents and the way they treat the child. Many parents are reluctant to admit their responsibility for their children's condition, as it automatically raises guilt within them. And since "guilty" is the word that they use to judge their parents, they are terrified that their children will feel the same about them. For the same reason, they are quick to attribute the child's condition to reasons beyond their control, such as a neuropsychiatric disorder that was influenced by genetic, environmental, or biochemical factors. Only when parents learn to replace the word "guilty" with "responsible" and stop being afraid of the truth will the healing begin.

Destructive Defense Mechanisms

A child doesn't have the ability to handle the kind of complex situations I've described. But since most children have to deal with them anyway, there are some automatic defense mechanisms they tend to adopt.

Repression

One of the ways children tend to cope with painful emotions in the absence of proper guidance is to repress them. Many adults don't remember long periods of their childhood; others developed a thick armor that keeps their feelings numb.

Some consciously decide at a young age that they will never need anyone. They often become independent and ambitious adults who face difficulties in creating intimacy and are reluctant to ask for support, as they perceive it as a weakness.

Others, fearing to experience rejection, become judgmental and offensive themselves. They are quick to declare that nothing can touch them, but the aggressiveness they demonstrate every time they "smell" rejection is a testimony to their pain. Like a spiny fruit with a sweet filling, deep down inside they are gentle and sensitive and yearn for love. Their stiff appearance and aggressive behavior, though, attract judgment and rejection instead.

Natural emotions that have been repressed tend to fester and impair our physical and emotional health. And, when instead of simply acknowledging them, we create a victim-villain narrative around what has happened, our pain magnifies.

Taking on the Role of the "Adult"

Some children try to take care of parents who fail to take care of themselves or siblings who are not receiving proper care. But even when the child manages to handle the situation and support the running of the household, he cannot fix the dysfunction of the family. And after stepping into the role of the "adult," the child will not be easily excused. Those who benefit from it will manipulate him and make him feel guilty for even thinking about stepping down.

Such a child becomes an adult who carries a lot of anger and guilt—anger about the helplessness of the adults in his life, and guilt about wanting to give up the obligation he took upon himself. As taking care of others becomes part of his identity, as a grown-up he may find himself in this position in romantic relationships, with friends, and at work. On the one hand, this role is his source of power, but on the other hand, it's his (or her) biggest source of pain.

Becoming a Parent-Pleaser

Parent-pleasing aims to win the parent's love and approval by trying to adjust to his or her expectations. Children who adopt this tactic believe that eventually the parent will notice how good they are. But since the attempt to please others involves self-disrespect, it achieves the opposite outcome and gains disrespect from the parent.

Parent-pleasers often turn into bitter people-pleasers, who tend to complain about not being appreciated and about those who don't put in as much effort as they do.

Defiance and Rebellion

Most children who are treated badly by their parents try at some point to stand up to them. They may defy, rebel, or find other ways to hurt their parents. Some do it at a young age; others try first to please the parents and only when they understand that it's useless, they change their approach.

But when a parent-child relationship turns into a battle, the situation only escalates and produces painful counter-reactions. In this bloody battle it's often the children who hurt and even mistreat the parents, especially when they grow up and gain power.

Numerous adults' lives are still led by such battle, and the feelings it creates damage every aspect of their lives.

Criticism and Shame

Many children are embarrassed by their parents' insufficient education, race, behavior, financial situation, or age. They feel their parents are inferior to others, often because the parents judge themselves this way. Sometimes one parent constantly degrades the other, and the children side with him or her against the other parent.

When a child feels ashamed of his parents, he may try to differentiate himself from them in order to emphasize his superiority. But since the attempt is based on negation and contempt toward the parents and their ways, it only strengthens the child's fear—that despite everything, he (or she) is inferior and faulty just like them.

At times, only after a parent is gone, can we understand the meaning of our actions, often finding it hard to forgive ourselves, even when we understand we did our best in dealing with a complicated situation.

Offensive and Violent Behavior

Children are not born bad or violent; they are simply born with the need for a stable adult to lean on and for unconditional love. When they don't get what they need, they start, at an early stage, to do what most adults do on a regular basis—look for an alternative that will provide them with a sense of power. Forceful or violent behavior toward family members or at school might satisfy the need.

As children at elementary school, we used to make fun of the unpopular kids. I used to take part in it and, sadly, really enjoyed it. It was amusing and gave me a sense of power. As an adolescent, I found myself on the other side when I became a target of bullying. Only then did I understand the consequences of my actions.

For many years I was carrying anger toward those who mocked me. Today I understand that a distorted need for power, born out of pain and low self-esteem, was what driven their actions. My fear of them and feelings of inferiority made me an easy target.

Cutting Ties with Family Members

It is not uncommon to see people cutting ties with close family members. The painful emotions created during childhood are not easily forgotten, and the rupture might deepen around recurring feelings of rejection, inheritance issues, or the need to take care of an elderly parent. Many feel it's better this way. "I don't have the energy for this anymore," they say. And though few will admit it, the real meaning of the sentence "I don't have the energy for this" is "I can't stand another disappointment. I can't deal again with the feeling that I'm not good enough. I can't bear this pain anymore."

When we cut ties with family members who hurt us, we enjoy immediate relief, but in the long run such an act intensifies the pain by creating a constant feeling of loss. The opponents hardly ever admit the pain; only their anger implies they still care. And even when their words say, "I don't care anymore," or, "I feel nothing," you can hear the anger as well as the longing in their voices and see it on their faces. From time to time reconciliation happens, but unless one of the sides lets go of blame toward the other, the dispute will sooner or later flare up again.

Those who adopt the tactic of cutting ties in order to avoid pain, find themselves using it hastily. Initially they use it with family members, then with friends, and eventually with their own children. As they cut more and more people out of their lives, their pain and loneliness become unbearable.

Breaking the Circle of Pain

The story of parents and children is the story of human pain—the story about children who suffer pain at the hands of their parents and pass it on to their own.

Does it mean that our parents are to blame, or that we'll have to carry the consequences of their actions for a lifetime? No. The circle of pain can be healed. The ones who can do it are those who can heal their own pain so they don't pass it on. And though many claim their relationships with their parents are not an issue anymore, few are those who brought real acceptance and forgiveness into those relationships.

There are a few steps to be taken in order to heal the circle of pain. Let's have a look at them.

Acknowledging the Emotions That Are Still There

The initial and crucial step toward healing is to acknowledge the emotions that we still carry. Despite claims such as "It doesn't bother me anymore," suppressed emotions can be easily identified through an angry tone of voice, sarcastic comments, or humor that covers pain.

Some adults never dared to admit anger or judgment toward their parents. If they are asked about their childhood, they are in a hurry to say that everything was great. Too ideal descriptions indicate that the adult expressing them is still driven by childish emotions that consider acknowledging the parents' weaknesses a betrayal.

Since those unspoken emotions are the source of all symptoms we experience as adults—struggles with relationships, career, or parenting; anger; stress; anxiety; self-judgment; and low self-esteem—whoever seeks a real solution to his or her problems will eventually have to acknowledge his or her true feelings. As long as they are denied, the same patterns will show up again and again in his or her life.

Letting Go of Unrealistic Expectations

Listen carefully to an adult who says, "I've already accepted who my parents are," and often you will hear anger and frustration in his voice. The nature of the conflicts a person still has with his parents and the pain those conflicts create imply that he did not accept the fact that they couldn't become the parents he (or she) expects them to be.

Unrealistic expectations exist despite rational understanding of the situation. Most adults, especially those who've been to therapy or are highly self-aware, understand what they can expect from their parents. When feelings of anger and frustration still show despite this understanding, they try to convince themselves why they shouldn't feel this way. But their efforts are futile, as the one demanding the parents to be who they should be is a small child who still lives within and demands what he feels is deserved—and that child doesn't want to understand. That's why, for any child, at any age, the hardest thing to accept is the fact that he will never get the love and support desired from his parents, and have the mother or father he (or she) dreamed of.

Thus, when I tell my clients that for the sake of their happiness and peace of mind they have to stop looking for their parents to change, they always resist it, though they have known their parents and what they are capable of for twenty, thirty, and even forty years. The thinking mind overlooks the enormous misery created by the futile argument with the facts and claims, "But how can I accept such a thing?" And the answer is, simply because it's a fact.

Becoming the Parent You Wanted to Have

"You're alive and safe, and I will not let any evil befall you. And you know that you can trust me. Because I love you."

At her words, my throat closed up and choked me. I wondered how she knew them to say. All my life, without knowing it, I had wanted someone to say those words to me, and have them be true and believable.

~ Robin Hobb, Fool's Fate

The longing for loving parental support is only natural, and deserving such support seems to be the inherent right of any living creature. But even in nature, due to the struggle for survival, not every offspring enjoys it. Most humans, however, do not enjoy such support, not due to lack of resources, and often despite love, abundance, and infinite attention. Because for the quote above to be real, the one expressing it should feel emotionally stable and whole in him- or herself—as someone who can confidently face the challenges of life, without paralyzing fear and without a silent cry for someone to save him or her.

The search for this protective figure is at the heart of humanity's suffering, but not for the obvious reason; the pain is not a direct outcome of our inherent right to unconditional love, protection, and support, but rather of the unrealistic expectation that someone will eventually make us feel whole by providing us with the love and support that we missed.

This expectation comes from the belief that only another person can fill the void within us, a belief that drives any child who grew up with a lack of unconditional love to desperately search for "the one who will always be there for me." Throughout this quest, each of us has moments when he feels as if he has finally achieved his goal and found the one he (or she) was always looking for. Its end, however, is always bound with disappointment. In romantic relationships bitter grudges quickly emerge around the expectation that our partner will always understand us, support us, and be willing at any given moment to put in his or her best effort to calm us down. Hence, an expectation for a relationship that carries parental characteristics, instead of an equitable relationship, the kind that is appropriate for two adults.

As long as we expect another person to make up for what we didn't receive in childhood and make us feel whole, on some level we keep seeing ourselves as children. That's why many adults feel as if they are still children and frequently allow themselves to act as poor children who deserve special treatment from others.

The problem with childish behavior is that in the short-term it often brings us what we want. When we demonstrate anger or sadness, it encourages those around us to make an effort to appease us. When we blame someone, he or she may feel the need to compensate us. The cute side of childish behavior makes us lovable and acts as an invitation to take care of us and protect us. And if we demonstrate helplessness, there will always be someone who sees it as an opportunity to come to our aid and become a hero for a moment. And thus, in many ways, such childish behavior gets us exactly what we always missed. So why am I still insisting that there is a problem with it? Because in the long term it creates the exact opposite; our current savior gets tired of treating our hurt feelings and feels offended when he or she finds out that we have no interest in his or her feelings, the constant drama tires even the most patient ones, and when we want those around us to take us seriously, we ignore the fact that we are the ones who taught them to treat us like children. And again we feel angry and sad.

If you ask those eternal children if it's not time to let go, they will say that maybe later, that being an adult is too hard, that everyone deserves to let go of responsibility from time to time. They will overlook the constant pain, the endless frustration, and the simple fact that allowing yourself to have fun like a child has nothing to do with being the "child" who demands that others take care of his feelings and compensate him for his (or her) miserable childhood.

Eventually, when all their efforts reach a dead end, some

wake up and realize that there is no one who can fill the void they feel within. And though this realization can be frightening, those who are willing to stop arguing with the facts find out that they are at the exact point they've been trying to reach all their lives. As, paradoxically, only when we let go of clinging to childhood and of the expectation that someone will compensate us for what we have experienced, do we suddenly realize that the parent figure we were always looking for is now within us.

Accepting the Love They Can Offer

Many children, even when they turn into adults and theoretically understand that their parents are doing their best, refuse to let go of the idea of how things are supposed to be; they are never satisfied with the amount of time their parents devote to them, with the way they prefer to spend time together, or with the topics they bring up. They cling to the childish idea of "the all-knowing and protective parent" and blame their parents: "They don't understand me," "They don't know how to support me," or, "We have nothing in common."

Yet it's not the intellectual level of the conversation or the life advice your parents can offer that determine the value you get from your relationships with them, but your ability to accept them as they are and enjoy the love they can offer.

Letting Go of the Attempt to Save Them

Sometimes what we find extremely challenging is to let our parents live their lives based on their wishes, without judging them for the suffering they are creating for themselves by their own hands. We look at them and realize how, with a few simple changes that are definitely within their reach (in our opinion), their lives could have looked completely different. "Anyone can change if they really want to," we insist and we try again to explain to them why they are wrong.

But sometimes the best help is to let go of the effort to help someone who doesn't want our help. The truth is that not everyone can change, and when we insist on helping, even if the other person eventually understands our reasoning, it will not compensate for the judgment he or she feels or for the bad atmosphere that judgment brings into the relationship.

When, metaphorically, we carry our parents on our shoulders, they become a burden to us. Then the effort to help them no longer comes from love. Instead, it becomes an attempt to break free from the burden we have laid on ourselves.

Forgiveness

Forgiving our parents and bringing acceptance into all we have experienced in childhood, no matter how painful it was, is the key to inner transformation. Without it, nothing can be achieved—no lasting change, no permanent release from pain, and no real peace of mind.

Forgiveness doesn't mean loving what happened; it simply means letting go of the blame we lay on others. This happens automatically when we are willing to accept that pain and unconsciousness have driven their actions, as well as to own our part in the situation. As when we stop complaining that "She doesn't treat me right," we find our own reflection in front of us—a person who yearns for our approval and love and reciprocates our feeling—hurting because he or she feels that we don't love and accept him or her. This is the paradox of human pain.

"But what about abuse, rejection, or abandonment?" you may ask. The pain of a child whose parents hurt him or her is heartbreaking. The fact that something like this can happen is unimaginable, yet it's still a part of our reality. That is why it's so important to understand that the person who did such things was so hurt that madness possessed him or her and controlled his or her actions. And when we understand that it's not personal, even to such situations we can bring forgiveness, if only internal.

Even though I have always loved my mother dearly, for many years I blamed her. I couldn't let go of the idea that if not for her character and the overprotective way she treated me, I would have been spared much pain. Some time ago when I looked at the old pictures, I saw a picture of her around the age of two, a picture of a small girl with big, sad eyes. Since then, at times when my mother acts childishly and unreasonably, I remember the little girl who felt that her mother never loved her enough, and I want to give her the feeling that she is completely loved exactly as she is. Not because I have to, not because I owe it to her, but simply because I can, because I love her.

Only when we no longer hold others accountable for our life circumstances, give up the victim mentality, and bring acceptance to everything that has happened in our lives, can we create the foundation for healing the vicious circle of pain.

It Is Never Too Late

Sometimes only after a parent is gone do we feel the need to heal the relationship, and the thought that it's too late might create a considerable amount of guilt and pain.

My father passed away when I was twenty-two. For years later, I felt huge guilt for what he had to suffer during the last years of his life, for the distance between us, and for judging and criticizing him. During his life I didn't always feel my love for him, and only when he was gone could I feel it again, and with it came the memory of the beautiful moments I shared with him as a child. And though I understood I was only a child who dealt with her own issues and couldn't do more for him, the guilt did not ease.

A few years after his death, my father began appearing in my dreams. Usually he was just present, not saying much, yet an integral part of the family. It made me realize that he is okay now, that he holds no anger, and that he is always with me. Through those dreams, I've managed to bring a sense of fulfillment to the relationship and to forgive myself.

Many find it hard to think of parents who are no longer with them, as their thoughts involve guilt for mistakes made and for moments missed, or self-pity for being left alone. But death is not the end of the story—even after a parent is gone, we can develop a new kind of relationship with him or her, based on the love that never dies, on the memory of beautiful moments shared, on forgiveness and acceptance of how things turned out.

Chapter 2

A Culture of Fear and Lack of Control

It's easy to manipulate a fearful and hurting person by promising him or her that certain achievements or possessions will bring him or her recognition and happiness. The emotional pain that passes from one generation to another and the belief system of our culture, ruled by fear and the idea of the individual's lack of control over his or her life, create the perfect setting for people to manipulate fellow humans in order to achieve power and fortune for themselves.

The Rule of Fear

If you think about it, you will find that fear is a central motive in your own life as well as in the lives of those around you—fear of getting sick or old, of war, of death, of not having enough, of not achieving what you want, or the fear that nothing will ever change.

Whereas natural fear is crucial for our survival, most of our fears come from a thinking methodology that was initially rooted by those who understood how to use fear to achieve power, fortune, and a sense of superiority. Today fear is further rooted by the good intentions of those driven by it, who believe it's an effective prevention mechanism, and, independently, by fear-based thought patterns. Fear has seized such control over our lives that it seems inevitable, the result of our circumstances, not something we have a choice about. Below are some examples of the way it's entrenched in our lives.

Setting Ourselves Toward Sickness

These days we are often encouraged to prepare ourselves for the moment we get sick. Let's, for example, examine the fight against breast cancer. In order to create awareness, words like battle and war are easily used. The widespread media coverage creates anxiety that affects more and more women at a younger and younger age, and too often overdiagnosis takes place, followed by unnecessary treatments. Could it be that the fearful campaigns, instead of helping, are increasing fear and expectations for the worst?

The medical establishment encourages us to believe that without medical examinations we have no way of knowing what is going on with our health. And when we accept this idea we learn to overlook the body's signals and distrust the body's healing power.

Long-term care insurance lays the ground for the day we will be old and won't be able to take care of ourselves. But is the way most people end their lives inevitable? Maybe if fear and emotional burdens hadn't eroded the human body so badly, we could have ended our lives much healthier and with a clearer mind.

Pharmaceutical companies have enormous power; they shrewdly sell us the need for one drug or another that promises to change the quality of our lives and solve all our problems. They fund studies that support the need for their drugs, pay for promotional articles, and create tempting marketing campaigns in which, for example, minor depression is presented as the "cold of the soul" and psychiatric drugs as the ultimate solution to this "distraction."[1] Using the enormous financial recourses they have, they make sure we believe in sickness, not in health.

Fear and Negativity Created by the News

News broadcasts are filled with local and national disasters. It's rare to see positive news, simply because it doesn't bring the same rating.

There is something addictive in the noisy and hectic way the news is presented, and many feel an exaggerated need to stay updated around the clock. They watch every news broadcast and read the newspapers; even during a vacation they cannot let it go.

The energetic frequency of fear and negativity transmitted by the news creates stress, anxiety, hopelessness, and despair.

Information Abundance—Is It Good for Us?

The abundance of information within our grasp is a wonderful thing, but it's also a breeding ground for those who have an interest in promoting certain ideas. It might lead to obsessive information-seeking and false self-diagnosis, and thus to anxiety.

One area in which this conflict shows is food marketing. Despite much evidence against the consumption of dairy products, for example, studies, often funded by those who have an interest in selling these products, support their consumption. The opponents, on their part, present their findings in an exaggerated way that causes unnecessary stress for those who consume dairy.

Many are afraid that the food they eat causes fatal diseases, that it's fattening, no matter in what quantity it is consumed, or that it's uncontrollably addictive. Instead of examining their bodies' reactions to a certain food, they are busy collecting more and more contradicting pieces of nutritional information, trying every new diet that pops up in the market, and living in constant fear. In practice, the body of an emotionally stable person will make the most of even the poorest nutrition, whereas the body of an emotionally stressed person cannot fully absorb even the healthiest of foods.

The Conspiracy of Silence

The conspiracy of silence is the way in which social conventions, without a guiding hand, maintain the rule of fear. Many believe that they are different from the rest and that something is wrong with them. When they look around and listen to others, it seems that everyone else is doing better, as most people go to great lengths to make sure things look good on the surface. For that purpose, they deny their true feelings, hide details that might make them look bad, and even distort the truth.

The Lack of Control Deception

Common spiritual teachings emphasize our inner source of power and our ability to consciously choose our path in life. Those teachings present the essential truth of human nature, yet they are incomplete, as they ignore the enormous power of the fundamental beliefs of our culture, among which is the belief of man's lack of control over his life.

Before we can become the masters of our lives, we should first identify those beliefs and shed light on their falsehood.

Psychiatric Diagnoses

These days people are quick on the trigger and easily adopt various diagnoses for themselves and their children, such as, "What can I do, I'm hot-tempered," "My kid has an anxious personality," or, "I have undiagnosed ADHD/OCD." Each diagnosis, either done by a professional or independently, turns quickly into the way they perceive themselves and their ability to make changes in their lives.

However, most behavioral patterns people consider to be personality traits are nothing but the symptoms of the major epidemics of our time—emotional pain, fear, and feelings of worthlessness. "Personality traits" such as pessimism or anxiety, for instance, are mainly an expression of a deeply entrenched thought pattern that projects itself into the future, automatically predicts the worst, and reacts to it as if it was a fact. When we learn to recognize the lie behind our thoughts, the pattern we considered to be a personality trait changes.

What psychiatry defines as "personality disorders" are simply more acute expressions of the thinking and emotional patterns that rule our culture. Paranoid Personality Disorder, for example, is, according to the DSM-5[2] (the manual of mental disorders of the American Psychiatric Association), characterized by "a pervasive distrust and suspiciousness of others such that their motives are interpreted as malevolent, beginning by early adulthood and present in a variety of contexts, as indicated by four (or more) of the following:

(1) Suspects, without sufficient basis, that others are exploiting, harming, or deceiving him or her.
(2) Is preoccupied with unjustified doubts about the loyalty or trustworthiness of friends or associates.
(3) Is reluctant to confide in others because of unwarranted fear that the information will be used maliciously against him or her.
(4) Reads hidden demeaning or threatening meanings into benign remarks or events.
(5) Persistently bears grudges, i.e., is unforgiving of insults, injuries, or slights.
(6) Perceives attacks on his or her character or reputation that are not apparent to others and is quick to react angrily or to counterattack.
(7) Has recurrent suspicions, without justification, regarding fidelity of spouse or sexual partner."

In practice, most of us experience these symptoms to a certain extent, and many who are perceived as normal by society would easily be able to identify four or more of them in their lives. Is it possible, then, that such a high portion of us suffer Paranoid Personality Disorder? Or perhaps, when we learn to identify the destructive thinking and emotional patterns that currently prevail throughout our society and go beyond them, the "disorder" will change?

In order to identify Dependent Personality Disorder, which is characterized by the DSM-5 as "a pervasive and excessive need to be taken care of that leads to submissive and clinging behavior and fears of separation, beginning by early adulthood and present in a variety of contexts, as indicated by five (or more) of the following:

(1) Has difficulty making everyday decisions without an excessive amount of advice and reassurance from others.
(2) Needs others to assume responsibility for most major areas of his or her life.
(3) Has difficulty expressing disagreement with others because of fear of loss of support or approval. (Note: Do not include realistic fears of retribution).
(4) Has difficulty initiating projects or doing things on his or her own (because of a lack of self-confidence in judgment or abilities rather than a lack of motivation or energy).
(5) Goes to excessive lengths to obtain nurturance and support from others, to the point of volunteering to do things that are unpleasant.
(6) Feels uncomfortable or helpless when alone because of exaggerated fears of being unable to care for himself or herself.
(7) Urgently seeks another relationship as a source of care and support when a close relationship ends.
(8) Is unrealistically preoccupied with fears of being left to take care of himself or herself."

Here too we can see widespread behavior and thought patterns; many would be able to identify five or more of them in their lives. They are expressions of the exaggerated need for approval and support that comes from fear of rejection and failure, and from a futile attempt to cling to childhood in order to make up for the lack of unconditional love we've experienced.

Sometimes an official diagnosis such as ADHD carries relief when it provides a scientific explanation for our faults and mistakes. However, when the family dynamics of a diagnosed child are thoroughly examined, one may wonder if the disorder the child suffers from could be separated from the deep emotional pain that he or she carries, caused by the parents' mental and emotional health, their relationships with the child, and the atmosphere at home. Due to these factors, fear, anger, and self-doubt overwhelm the child, making it impossible for him or her to concentrate, and trigger the extreme behavior typical of this disorder. The parents' reluctance to acknowledge their personal responsibility for the child's condition may push them to seek an official diagnosis for his or her condition.

Despite the fact that over sixty years have passed since the "chemical imbalance theory"* was presented, it has not been confirmed to this day. For many, though, this is not an obstacle for using it as a justification to prescribe psychiatric drugs to a child or an adult.

Around the age of thirty, when I decided to deal with the emotional pain I felt I had been carrying for too long, I turned to psychotherapy. When I said I was angry, the psychologist swiftly recommended antidepressants. I had no doubt that this was not an appropriate solution for me, and I didn't consider it even for a moment. I felt a strong inner knowing that there are better ways to deal with the situation, and my determination paid off. I found different, more effective, ways

---

* The "chemical imbalance theory" proposed that mental disorders are caused by a chemical imbalance in the brain.

to treat myself, and today the pain and the anger that were part of my life for many years are gone. Many, though, are easily tempted to take "just a little pill that even if it doesn't help, it can't do any harm," and within an instant lose faith in their ability to support themselves.

Another expression of the belief that humans lack control over their lives is the approach of the medical establishment to mental health conditions and addiction. Health professionals often say that if you suffer from an eating disorder, it will always be a part of your life, even if dormant at times. My personal experience, however, proves otherwise; throughout adolescence I suffered from bulimia for eight years. At twenty-three, as a result of a change I made in my life, I overcame it completely, all by myself. If I did it, so can others. It is probable that if the establishment's assumption was that overcoming eating disorders is a standard, the public's assumption would change accordingly and so would their results.

Some of my clients were told by professionals that due to their personality structure they will never be happy—the same "personality structure" I used to have. And someone I know, who was diagnosed with bipolar disorder, has "miraculously recovered" after letting go of resentment and self-pity.

Maybe if you believe it is possible, you will find that your condition is reversible too.

Spirituality, Fate, and Luck

Spiritual teachings that label us as one type of personality or another also assume that we lack control over our lives. In a mysticism program on Israeli television, a numerologist analyzed a listener's problem based on her date of birth. "She is an 8. She's like fire. She can't control it," he explained.

Such teachings assume that the source of our problems is congenital or that we are influenced by factors we can't control. But this is never the case—the source of all that we experience is within us. At any given moment we can check our thoughts, beliefs, emotions, and behavior in order to create change in our lives. The focal point is always the now, and any influence from the past has an expression that can be identified and dealt with at the present moment.

The belief in fate, luck, and the evil eye also assumes our lack of control over our lives and contradicts the fact that we are the ones creating our own reality. Within the framework of life circumstances over which we have no control (what's called fate), the freedom of choice is infinite. "Unfortunate luck" is an event or a sequence of events that reflects our emotional state and beliefs, and the evil eye can impact us only if we believe in it.

The term "subconscious" adds to that and provides alleged scientific validity to the collective belief in the individual's lack of control over his or her life. It is true that before we become conscious and aware there are many things we are not aware of, but we can always develop greater awareness. Instead of saying things such as, "Maybe I have subconscious fears," listen to your thoughts and you will find what triggers your feelings, what your real motives are, and what you really want.

Treating Humans as Weak, Easily Influenced Creatures

Society itself validates the lack of control assumption by

treating humans, especially young people, as creatures who lack control, are easily influenced, and who cannot, therefore, make wise choices on their own. But even though many of us do make destructive choices, it's not due to a lack of information or judgment.

Like any other life form on the planet, we are designed to prevent self-harm; the body responds to toxicity by feeling sick and emitting the toxins, and alerting us when we have overeaten by giving us a stomachache and nausea. Our emotions, too, are a wise mechanism that provides us with feedback on what's right or wrong for us by making us feel good or bad.

In a state of emotional balance, lack of control won't be a problem even in the face of temptations, as the unpleasant sensations serve as a natural balance mechanism. But when all we are looking for is a moment of relief from our burning emotions, painful thoughts, and feelings of worthlessness, we are likely to use anything that provides such a relief, no matter the consequences.

Oppression, Enslavement, and Hierarchy

All humans are created equal, yet most of us believe that for some reason or another we are less than others or superior to them.

Oppression and enslavement are social patterns in which one person or a group of people derives benefits and a sense of power by exploiting others. They learn to believe they are superior to fellow humans and find it hard to see others as equal or even as humans at all. And those who are treated as inferiors—although they might protest against it—accept the idea of their inferiority and carry it throughout generations, until individuals who are willing to risk their reputation, their freedom, and even their lives, dissolve the illusion of inferiority and bring about a change. They pave the way for those who come next, who can now, due to the change in their self-perception, achieve goals that were impossible for their group before.

The Worship of Knowledge

The worship of academic and scientific knowledge is another factor that makes us doubt ourselves and the idea that we can gain knowledge by sensing and exploring the world around us. Because of it we might, for example, agree without question with a diagnosis given by a physician or a psychiatrist and overlook our gut feeling that the diagnosis is insufficient or incorrect.

Frequent cases of malpractice and false diagnoses may become a wake-up call for those who are ready to open their eyes.

Life Advisors—Do They Really Help Us?

The numerous life advisors and specialists that have become so popular these days serve as another channel through which we revoke our power and internal authority. While there's nothing wrong with getting expert advice when needed, the answers for our lives are always within. When we seek advice for every aspect of our lives, whether from a professional or a friend, it becomes impossible for us to listen to our own voices and trust ourselves.

While a financial advisor may easily explain why it doesn't make sense for a mother of scant means to buy a television for her son simply because he wants to have one in his room, the advisor will find it hard to answer her irrational need to compensate the child for being the target of her frustration or for the absence of his father from his life. Relationship specialists who advise us on how to behave to attract love, overlook the inability of a person suffering from emotional burnout to control his or her reactions. And seeking the advice of parenting gurus, instead of helping, often makes parents doubt themselves and distrust their natural instincts.

Holy Scripture Commentary

Holy Scripture commentary is a fundamental source for both fear and the belief that we lack control over our lives. Though all religions are based on love and include the necessary guidelines for a life of health, happiness, and abundance, many of the commentaries given to the Holy Scriptures over the centuries create fear of negative reward, derive guilt, and justify violence and hatred.

In the light of the different religions, as interpreted, the worthlessness of man is emphasized in the face of the mighty God, and the need to comply with a cleric's dictations without question suggests that ordinary people lack the ability to make moral decisions on their own. Many commentaries assume the superiority of one group of human beings over another, and often humans are perceived as helpless, as beings who are constantly torn between Satan and God.

Chapter 3

Who Is Running the Show of Your Life?

Destructive thought patterns, limiting beliefs, and emotional pain are living within us as parasites that spread fear and pain. They control our feelings, thoughts, and perceptions—and thus, control the show of our lives.

Over-Sensitivity

Most people confuse true sensitivity—the ability to feel deeply, express emotions, and show compassion toward another—with over-sensitivity—the tendency to interpret almost every word or act as malicious, and thus be quick to take offense and have a dramatic reaction.

Contrary to popular belief, over-sensitivity is not an innate trait, and by handling our emotions correctly we can overcome it and reveal the enormous power of true sensitivity.

The first step to becoming free from over-sensitivity is to

identify the moments in which it takes charge:

- Sometimes a relatively minor event can awaken intense pain and a reaction that seems disproportionate to the situation. When it happens, you may judge yourself severely for your irrational reaction and for being so offended by something that seems so insignificant. In such moments you are unaware of the fact that the event has awakened residue of similar pain you have experienced in the past. For example, a person's dismissive tone of voice echoes your parents' tone of voice. Thus, you are not reacting to the event itself but to an accumulation of old emotional pain that still lives in you. "Something inside me exploded," explained a client after erupting with rage toward a perceived disrespect from her daughter. At such moments the pain that arises may be so intense that it blinds you and makes you hear things that weren't said. Forgiveness toward yourself is the key to breaking free from this pattern—as when you judge yourself harshly, your pain intensifies, and with it the lack of control over your emotions.
- You expect people to treat you as the center of the universe—to comfort you, make you happy, and meet all your needs—and you feel pain, disappointment, and rage when they fail to do so. When someone acts like this, it's because he or she demands those around to treat him or her in a parental manner, in an attempt to compensate for the lack of unconditional love.
- You might get impatient, offended, and angry when someone else is at the center of attention.
- Door-slamming"—In the face of certain events, you may suddenly feel a rush of anger and sharp emotional pain, along with a strong impulse to run away from the

situation by slamming the phone or leaving hastily without explanation.

- Recreating your "personal shell shock"—My biggest pain as a child was that people preferred my twin sister over me. For years I feared that the men in my life would find her more attractive or either choose someone else, prettier or younger, over me. Again and again, in different areas of my life, I recreated the situation of being the second best—worthy but not enough to stand first. Even after this pattern has almost dissolved from my life, it still recurs in my dreams from time to time, creating intense pain, frustration, and rage.

Raging Emotional Pain

Residues of emotional pain that was initiated in childhood and intensified by different events we have experienced throughout life are creating an energy field that lives within us. This energy is kept alive, even when we don't think about the painful events, as long as we regret the past and hold other people accountable for what happened to us. When a new event echoes with the old energy, huge pain arises and takes control of our thoughts, emotions, and reactions.

This destructive "entity" of emotional pain may be identified by the following:

- You find yourself wallowing in melancholy about yourself and your life circumstances, unwilling to acknowledge the good in your life, and insisting that everyone else's situation is better and that no one has been through such difficulties, while deliberately overlooking the facts.

- You feel the need to hurt yourself and prove how worthless you are. You harshly judge your looks and dismiss your achievements.
- You feel uncontrollable anger along with an urge to pick a fight, to complain about and blame others, the circumstances, and the world, along with a sense of victimhood and compulsion to interpret the situation in a negative way and take things out of context. When you hear your partner saying again and again, "But it's not what I said," or, "This is not what I meant," try to see if the pain in you has awakened and distorted your perception.
- You feel the urge to run away from your painful emotions and disturbing thoughts by using distractions that may easily turn into an addiction—food, television, sex, screens, alcohol, drugs, work, or obsessive relationships.

Running Away from Your Feelings of Worthlessness

The feeling that I'm not worthy enough as I am is something that almost anyone these days carries to a certain extent. It lives within us and manages our lives with an iron fist so that we all make considerable efforts to enhance our self-esteem and sense of worthiness or to keep them from harm. Unfortunately, the strategies we tend to use only increase the feeling that despite our achievements we are not worthy enough.

In order to avoid these destructive strategies, you must first learn to identify them:

- You might try to elevate your self-esteem and the way you are perceived by others by acquiring status symbols, such as academic degrees, possessions, or career success, not necessarily out of joy but out of a desire to be accepted and fear of feeling inferior to others.

- You seek friendship with those you perceive as superior to you, due to the belief that relationships with such people add to your prestige and self-esteem.
- You invest time and effort in keeping your self-image intact—you avoid doing things that might end in failure, sometimes you lie to avoid possible judgment and rejection, you make efforts to be perceived as a good person and to be loved by everyone, and you are reluctant to admit your mistakes.
- You may derive enjoyment from dealing with someone else's problems, faults, and mistakes, and might find yourself expressing contempt, complaining about, and blaming others without taking responsibility for your own actions. If you are honest with yourself, you will find that such acts supply a momentary feeling of righteousness and superiority.
- Upon "rational thinking," if I did something wrong and I judge myself for it, my judgment toward myself makes amends for what I did and confirms that I'm a moral person ("I cannot forgive myself for that," "I deserve to suffer"). But beating yourself up for your mistakes, unlike the willingness to learn from them, does not fix anything; it drains your energy, affects your self-esteem (as it makes you feel faulty and wrong), and creates paralyzing fear of self-punishment in case of future mistakes.
- Turning someone into an enemy—a driver on the road, a neighbor, a co-worker, a parent, or a life partner. Perceiving him as vicious, interpreting his actions as an act of assault, and, as a consequence, condemning and showing hostility

toward him, while emphasizing your personal and moral superiority to his (or hers).
- Conducting wars of justice and involvement in continual lawsuits—though usually around money, such battles are often driven by the urge to regain trampled dignity through retribution.
- Dehumanization—the tendency to treat others as less than humans: humans of another race, religion, gender, or sexual orientation. Those who have different political views, the ones who harmed us, or the ones who have money and nothing allegedly touches them. Dehumanization is so deeply entrenched in our culture that when the news anchor reports an accident in which three were killed, and then adds "from…" (the name of an Arab village), the Jewish listener feels relieved, simply because he or she was raised to believe that they are the bad ones and we are the good ones. Yet the ability to see the humanity of others is quickly forgotten on a daily basis—in a moment of rage toward a service provider or the ones we love most. Dehumanization serves as a justification for hatred and violence toward others
- Violence toward other life forms is an act of aggression that doesn't recognize the shared life source of all living beings. When a child demonstrates violence toward an animal, it's not because he or she is inherently bad, but because the child is surrounded by energy of violence and negativity and because he or she feels small.

You might find some of the above descriptions objectionable, as no one wishes to see him- or herself as selfish, arrogant, or immoral. That's why some will deny behaving this way or present their behavior as an inevitable reaction to circumstances. But these are simply culture-based behavioral patterns used to alleviate feelings of fear and inferiority, and acknowledging them is the first step toward freedom.

∴

As long as we are driven by feelings of worthlessness and emotional pain—dissatisfaction and fear will run our lives no matter what we achieve.

The pain and the fear are sustained by limiting beliefs, useless coping mechanisms, and destructive thought patterns. They are so cleverly entangled in our culture that seeing them naked and identifying the lie in them is almost impossible, until we wake up.

PART TWO

Awakening

Chapter 4

Awaken from the Bad Dream

What Is Awakening?

Awakening is the recognition of the madness of the human mind. The understanding that all problems mankind faces are rooted in the thought patterns of our culture, and that there might be another way.

If you look inside and around you, you may notice that human suffering has reached a tipping point and impacts even young children these days. Most of us are driven by painful emotions caused by identification with the thinking mind: anger, resentment, and regrets about the past, fear of the future, and dissatisfaction with our life circumstances.

One of the most significant experiences I've ever had was a misunderstanding that taught me how delusional I was. One day, a few years ago, I thought that a promise given to me was broken and that someone else was going to take my place. I was deeply offended, but after giving it some thought I decided, despite everything, to forgive the promise-giver. A few more days passed and in order to clear the atmosphere between us, I decided to tell him why I was angry with him and that I'd already forgiven. During our conversation, I was shocked to learn that the entire chain of events I'd built in my mind had nothing to do with what really happened. That is, I was angry and had forgiven him for something that never happened.

Assuming we know what other people think, feel, or how they intend to react, is a common mistake. We make hasty assumptions, yet the painful emotions they create are real, as if what we have imagined already happened.

At the heart of the awakening process is the realization that we often see the world the same way as an anorectic girl sees her body—in a distorted perception, derived from the pain of the past, which we blindly project into the future while expecting more of the same. A perception that has little to do with the facts.

Are You Already Awakening?

Spiritual awakening is not something you can achieve if it's not already happening to you on some level. And how will you know if it does? There is no clear-cut answer, but there are a few signs you may see in your life:

- When you begin to awaken, you realize that things do not just happen to you by coincidence (people's reactions to you or recurring circumstances).
- You are willing to admit your faults, instead of only noticing others', and understand that in order to change your life you should first change yourself.
- Though you still want to achieve certain goals, you understand that without changing your inner state no external circumstances can make you happy for long.

- You are able to listen to your inner voice beyond social conventions and the words of authority figures.
- You don't have a guru, and you are not following a path that requires obedience.
- You can identify the "movies" created by the thinking mind, and though they still affect you emotionally, you don't fully believe them.
- You understand that despite the reluctance to fully face the truth, things won't disappear through suppression and denial.
- You no longer expect the world to adapt to you, and instead of resisting your life circumstances, you begin working with them.
- You understand that no matter how far you run, you cannot run away from yourself.

The Three Foundations of Awakened Life

The synonyms awakening, spiritual awakening, and enlightenment have been interpreted in many different ways, mostly spiritual. However, it is the earthly aspects of the awakening process that are essential for a life of happiness and choice.

Awakened, conscious life has three fundamental characteristics, as described below.

Clarity

When we start to awaken, we feel as if dark and distorting eyeglasses have been removed from our eyes. We identify the pain and the madness around us and understand that this is the reason for what people do to each other, to the environment, and to other life forms, not what's called evil. We realize that we, as well, hurt, and maybe still are hurting, others when we're in the grip of our pain.

Before we understand how deep human unconsciousness is, we expect everyone to act rationally and take offense when someone doesn't keep his or her word, uses personal information against us, or keeps hurting us despite recurring requests to stop. But when an unconscious person promises in a moment of clarity that he or she will never repeat his or her harmful behavior, it's the same as when a violent man promises his wife he will never hit her again.

The following behaviors are some of the indications of human unconsciousness: presenting irrational arguments in an exaggerated way that does not reflect the truth, bringing up past events that presumably had been forgiven and tying them in a twisted way to current events, denying things that were said or done in the past, judging others for the same things the person him- or herself does, unwillingness to acknowledge the consequences of his or her actions, defending oneself even before being criticized, and seeing oneself as an innocent victim while laying the blame on others.

Even if in a rare moment an unconscious person acknowledges his or her mistakes, it won't be long before he or she denies them again.

When we understand the nature of human unconsciousness, as well as the fact that unconscious people cannot control their feelings and reactions even if they want to, compassion arises, and instead of wasting energy in an attempt to make such people understand their mistakes, we focus on setting boundaries where they are needed.

Inner Authority

Inner authority (the ability to listen to our inner direction and be true to our hearts) starts with the understanding that any person or teaching that preaches we are lacking knowledge or are faulty by birth is a tool in the hands of those who have an interest in keeping us under the control of fear, even if unconsciously.

When inner authority is awakened within a person, it makes him or her question everything before he or she fully understands it, even if it was said by a highly regarded professional, a specialist on a television show, a married friend, or a rich guy.

Another aspect of the awakening of inner authority is the willingness to trust the innate knowledge that always guides us through our inner voice, feelings, and intuition, but that we rarely listen to.

You might think that inner authority can lead to chaos and anarchy, a situation where people are doing whatever they want and only looking out for their own interests. But a closer look will tell you that this is actually the current situation. When our minds are clear we can see the connection between our actions and the results we are getting, and notice how by hurting others we end up hurting ourselves as well. This is the balancing mechanism of nature that allows all life forms, except humans, to live alongside each other in balance and harmony.

Personal Responsibility

Personal responsibility is the basis of conscious creation. It's the understanding that we are the ones creating every aspect of our reality—the people around us, their reaction to us, the circumstances of our lives, what we achieve, and what we don't. All is our creation.

True, it's mainly an unconscious creation, but it's still ours. Thus, we can change it when we learn to examine the facts without judgment, listen to our thoughts and our covert feelings, and examine the relationship between our actions and the outcomes we get.

The key to consciously creating our reality lies in the answer to the question we can answer anytime no matter how random the circumstances seem and how obvious the guilt of the other person appears to be. "How did I create that?" meaning, what in my behavior, reactions, expectations, inner energy, and the way I treat myself brought me the results I'm having, either good or bad?

Simple Yet Profound Change

A fundamental belief held by many is that profound transformation requires time and effort. You may hear this belief hiding behind statements such as, "What comes easy goes easy," "It doesn't count if I didn't make an effort," or, "To be a spiritual person is hard work." There is a glorification of difficulty and suffering.

Self-enhancement can also be derived from perceiving oneself as problematic or complicated. Examine if the following statement creates a feeling of subtle superiority within you: "My problems are deep-rooted; some hocus-pocus won't solve them." Addressing ourselves in this way enables us to buy more time before giving up the behavioral patterns we complain about while enjoying the benefits they provide.

When we begin to awaken, things start to happen effortlessly; obstacles that previously seemed insurmountable dissolve, painful events from our past become an old story, self-defeating behaviors suddenly change, and anger that might have been there for years disappears when we understand its cost. The change is quick, profound, and, mainly, easy.

Such transformation requires no struggle in order to preserve the outcomes, and involves no need "to work on ourselves" or to live under a strict reign. Though naturally, as in any transformation process, from time to time the old patterns come alive and it seems as if everything we have achieved is lost. The awakening consciousness is not yet established and should be strengthened like a muscle we have never used before. Initially, we notice the impact of our actions only in retrospect; later, simultaneously; and eventually, before we act or react.

Chapter 5

Being: The Magical Dimension of Life

The power of thought was given to humans to be used as a compass. To encourage creativity, God did not give humans control over their thoughts; he did, however, give them the ability to observe their minds. "Thoughts will evoke emotions, which, in turn, will remind you to examine your thoughts. Eventually, your thoughts will become a physical reality that reflects the content of your minds. And when you get tired of the game of thought, you can always reunite with me and rest without thought."
~ From *"The Five Wondrous Powers"*

The Failure of Modern-Age Thought Patterns

Rational thinking is an amazing ability that differentiates us from other species. It enables learning from past experience and planning future actions accordingly. If we had used it for its intended purpose, it would have been quite helpful. However, it lost direction and became compulsive, repetitive, and uncontrollable. Instead of supporting us it became the thing that keeps our pain alive and creates dissatisfaction and fear.

The essence of the thought pattern I have just described, which could be called "fear-based thinking," is obsessive engagement with the self and its problems.

When you learn to listen to your thoughts, you will find that you are hardly ever here and now, and that wherever your thoughts turn, they reach a dead end.

Past—A significant portion of our thinking deals with the past. Our minds are frequently occupied with thoughts about what could have happened if we had chosen differently, accompanied by painful imagined scenarios that cannot be proven wrong about where we could have been today and how everything could have been much better. With anger about things that happened; had they not, the thinking mind tells us, our lives would have looked completely different. With sorrow about choices we've made, about unutilized possibilities, or about words spoken. With longing for a sweet moment that we fear we will never experience again, or for people who are no longer in our lives. In retrospect the thinking mind prettifies the experience, glorifies the good and overlooks the bad, and we blame ourselves for not being wise enough to enjoy the moment.

The compulsive preoccupation with what happened and with the question "What if?" creates intense pain, burning anger, a sense of missing out, and despair. And when our thoughts dwell on the past it becomes a reality for us, and unconsciously we project it into the future, assuming it will look the same.

Future—Another hobby of the thinking mind is the future.

When the thinking mind turns to the future, it does one of the following:

It visualizes future events and automatically predicts the worst—how I'm going to be fired or how I'll remain lonesome without a life partner by my side. This thought pattern is frequently called pessimism; however, while pessimism is presumed to be a personality trait, what I describe here is an acquired thought pattern that is not a part of the personality.

Additionally, the thinking mind looks ahead, longing to reach the current goal on which our happiness depends: a romantic relationship, marriage, or a new job. But here, too, there is no joy, only fear that what we long for won't happen or that the accomplishment won't fulfill its aim. Out of this painful place, we try to hold on to something that will relieve the pain, if only for a moment, such as a romance, a vacation, or anything else that can create a temporary distraction. And when the primary goal is to get rid of our painful thoughts, we make hasty decisions that provide short-term relief, without thinking about the long-term implications they involve.

Further, the thinking mind tends to build detailed scenarios about events that may never happen: what I'm about to say, how the other person is about to react, how I'm about to feel, etc. Usually those scenarios involve confrontation and pain, and the emotional reaction is taking place at the present moment based on the imaginary scenario.

Present—Eventually the thinking mind turns to the present moment. When it assesses *what is*, except for rare moments of satisfaction, it treats the present moment as a transition period toward something better, and frequently as an obstacle or a problem.

Due to the illusion that in the future, when our wishes come true, everything will be much better and we will finally be able to start "truly living," the thinking mind does not consider the present moment to be valuable in itself.

The feelings related to the present moment are usually dissatisfaction, resentment, self-pity, and resistance to *what is*.

∴

As implied by its name, fear is the primary emotion associated with fear-based thinking—fear of missing out, fear that I've ruined my chances, and fear that nothing will ever change.

The Sabotaging Voice—Your Internal Enemy

The sabotaging voice is the voice of fear-based thinking. It's the voice that talks in our heads continuously, creating self-doubt, fear, self-judgment, and pain. It repeats offensive words that were said to us in the past, often by our parents. Words we are now using against ourselves because we believe them to be true, despite not wanting to.

The voice is a fan of popular statements that imply fear and limitations, such as "You better lower your expectations," "Always prepare for the worst," or, "Life is a compromise."

Under a cover of goodwill it always makes you feel bad about yourself. "Leave it; you have no chance to succeed," "Look, you are being mocked again," "Watch out; people will think you are crazy," or, "You just can't control yourself, can you?"

It likes to deceive us and say that the compliments we get are a lie. That if, for example, someone said something nice to us it's because he or she needs something or because his or her perception of reality is distorted. "They did it to you,"

"They took it away from you," it pushes us to feel offended and pick a fight. It knows us intimately, and just like our worst enemies it knows exactly where to push in order to hurt us.

You may try to reassure yourself against the harsh words with positive ones, but it's not that simple. The enormous energy of the sabotaging voice and our deep identification with its statements makes it almost impossible not to believe it. Almost.

Fixing the Thinking Failure with Additional Thinking

The way we tend to deal with the fear and the pain created by fear-based thinking is with additional thinking. "Rationalization" is not, as one may think, using rational thinking, but the attempt to defeat unwanted thoughts and emotions with rational arguments. We use it within ourselves, we ask those around us to use it to encourage us and soothe our fears, and we use it to advise others how to make decisions and handle their feelings.

Here are some examples of such "rational" arguments we tend to use:

- Why I should feel lucky for what I've achieved, despite feeling dissatisfied.
- Why the current situation is not as bad as it seems, and how it could have been much worse.
- Why, after all, I'm lucky for not making the decision that in retrospect feels like missing out. And why, despite not being happy with its results, the decision I've made is the best.
- Why there is no reason for me to feel what I feel (fear, jealousy, disappointment, or any other unwanted emotion).

∴ Why I am lucky that my partner left me (as he or she doesn't deserve me and only did me a favor).

Sometimes rationalization is no more than empty words prettifying the truth, but often it does reflect it. The truth, however, remains meaningless as long as we don't feel it within, and repeating the facts cannot change the way we feel.

If you look into it, you will find that despite the brief relief provided by using rationalization, instead of calming you down it amplifies the pain, as the attention given to the unwanted thoughts in an effort to disprove them implies they are real.

Since rationalization doesn't affect feelings, using it creates self-judgment that tells us something is wrong with us for not being able to adopt such a rational way of thinking.

Another popular technique is what's called "positive thinking." It's based on the same idea as rationalization—an attempt to replace the unwanted thoughts with positive ones. Positive thinking, too, unlike true positivity, about which we'll talk later, is often based on denial and pretense, and thus, the fear that the unwanted thoughts will return always remain in the background.

Only during the quiet moments that we couldn't avoid or late at night, when the incessant noise in our heads won't subside, do we stop denying the futility of those techniques.

Breaking Free from Identification with Our Thoughts

As long as we identify with our thoughts, fear rules our lives. Liberation begins when we understand that the thought pattern itself is false; referring to something that hasn't happen yet, even if it might, as a matter of fact, is a delusion. The assumption that everything would have been better had we chosen differently cannot be proven, and thus it's only an illusion. And the biggest deception, which time always proves wrong, is that our circumstances are the problem, and that once they change everything will finally be all right.

Becoming aware of the thought pattern and its deceptions, and of the compulsive need to hurt and punish ourselves, is by itself a powerful transformational tool. But in order to see things clearly without falling again into identification with the seemingly real delusion created by our thoughts, presence is needed.

The Ticket to Your New Life: Meet Presence

Presence in the moment,* in its basic essence, is an alert, focused break from thinking. Even though this description does not cover the depth of the realm of being, it can serve as a starting point.

When we say, "I must take some time off," or, "I've managed to truly unwind," we refer to the rare feeling that everything is as it should be; our worries disappear, the feeling of dissatisfaction that is always in the background is replaced with real enthusiasm and joy, fear clears the way, and for a moment we feel free, light, and content.

Such a feeling, achieved naturally, is a rare event for most of us. It usually happens only during a vacation, at the beginning of a romantic relationship, before fear takes over, or at the short moments after we've achieved something, before the sense of accomplishment dissolves. At such moments we tend to attribute the good feeling to the circumstances, though it's primarily the release from the burden of our

---

* Throughout the book the terms "presence in the moment," "presence," and "being," are used interchangeably.

minds. When someone is completely possessed by his or her thoughts, even a vacation on a magical beach in Thailand will not free him or her from the burden of his or her mind.

Some interpret the term "presence in the moment" as "live for the moment" and angrily react, "But I can't think only of myself and do whatever I want." Presence, however, is just the opposite; when we "live for the moment," we don't give a damn about anything or anyone; we ignore the outcomes of our actions and other people's feelings. When we are present we are attentive to ourselves and to others and take into consideration the consequences of our actions.

To be present means that when you are with your children you are really with them, not on your phone, and when you spend time with your mother you are with her, not in your head complaining about not having better things to do. And when you feel you can't be present with them, you respect them and yourself by taking time for yourself, instead of forcing yourself to do "the right thing."

To be present is to really see the beauty around—the flower at the side of the road, bright skies after the rain, or storks flying. It's to really hear—what the other person says, the emotions behind his or her words, what's not being said, not only the interpretations in your head.

To be present is to allow *what is*—whatever you are feeling, choices made against your will, current circumstances, or anything else that already is.

When we are present there is still room for aspirations and future plans. Those, however, will not be driven by pressure or fear. There is also a sense in exploring the past for the purpose of learning, as opposed to using it for self-judgment and futile thinking about what could have been "if only…."

The Practice of Presence

In order to become present it's not enough to make a decision to stop dealing with all the nonsense that occupies our minds. First we must learn how to free ourselves from the grip of fear-based thinking.

The following exercises are the simplest way to start bringing presence into your life and freeing yourself from unwanted thoughts:

1. Mindful breathing—Focus your attention on your breath. Feel the air moving in and out of the body, notice how it moves inside your body; the expansion of the chest and abdomen, and the flow of air through the nostrils. Focusing on the breath without judging it or trying to change its rhythm creates relaxation and expands inner space. It helps in creating a space between stimulus and response and in falling asleep when thoughts won't let go at night. It's a simple action that can be done at any time.

2. Listening—Be still for a few moments and listen to the sounds around you: driving cars, birds singing, a distant talk, or anything else. Sometimes you will hear pleasant sounds; other times, listening without judgment will increase your tolerance for unpleasant sounds.

3. Observation—Look at something carefully. It's better for it not to be something that triggers thoughts, such as another person, words, or an object that holds memories. When we learn to look at nature in this way, we find the magnificence of even a simple flower. However, since this exercise might create anticipation for a sense of awe, sometimes it's best to focus on meaningless objects, such as the surface of your desk.

4. Attentive touch—Touch something, no matter what, and feel its texture; when you wake up in the morning pay attention to the feeling of your body on the mattress; when you perform simple actions, such as turning the lights on or off, do it mindfully; while watching television, put your hands on your abdomen or chest and feel their warmth; close your lips gently and feel their softness.

You may use these four exercises or any one of them, upon your preference, from time to time during the day, for a second or a fraction of it (until thoughts pop in your mind, as the practice should be effortless). I don't mention how many times the practice should take place as the thinking mind might turn it into a trap and say, "I didn't practice enough," or, "I failed this," whereas even if you practice only once a day, it is more than you did before.

At the beginning it's best to practice when you are relatively calm; if you try to practice only when you are agitated, you will find it very challenging. But don't worry, each such small exercise expands your inner space, and in a relatively short time you will reap the fruits of your labor also in times of challenge.

You can use various events during the day as practice reminders. For example, when I wake up in the morning, before I get up, I pay attention to my body's position on the mattress; before I begin my workday I sit quietly for a moment, listening to the birds and looking out the window; when I sit in front of the computer I listen to the sounds around me from time to time; while walking down the street, I notice the young leaves, a tree, or a flower; and if disturbing thoughts keep me up at night, I turn my attention to my breathing.

Although presence allows us to quiet our minds, not every

activity that helps us to distract ourselves from thinking creates inner stillness. Staring or daydreaming, for instance, may look similar to presence, but they are not. Screen activities may take our minds off our problems and fears, but unlike presence, they do not create inner stillness, only a kind of apathy.

When I become present after I've been immersed in thoughts, I feel as if my eyes had literally moved back from the back of my head to their natural place. Everything becomes sharper, and it seems as if up to this moment I didn't really see what's around me.

Five Minutes of Stillness

I like to use the following exercise when I want to enhance presence, especially at moments of unease and agitation.

Find a quiet spot—it can be a pleasant room at your home, your garden, or any other place you find comfortable. Set the timer for five minutes and just sit quietly, with your eyes open or closed. Listen to the sounds, look attentively at what's around you, pay attention to your breathing and your body's sensations, and if thoughts arise, don't try to fight them. From time to time bring your attention back from thinking to what's around you. Feel the life around and inside you.

"Mega-Presence"

Like in the previous exercise, first find a quiet and pleasant spot. In this exercise it's better, but not necessary, to be outdoors.

Sit quietly, in a comfortable position; don't try to avoid

moving or thinking, but stay as present and alert as possible.

This exercise can be done for ten minutes, half an hour, or more. You can determine the duration in advance, or just sit until you feel serenity fills every corner of your body.

∴

By themselves, the basic presence exercises are no more than a brief relief from the burden of the thinking mind, but along with a clear understanding of the destructive patterns of fear-based thinking, they turn into a powerful key for change.

The Mind's Resistance to Presence

When you start practicing presence, you will likely have thoughts such as, "It's hard," "I don't have time for this," "How exactly is this supposed to help me?" or, "I can't just sit and do nothing!"

The thinking mind will do whatever it can to avoid presence, as it's not a coincidence that we are hardly ever present. The reason that most of the time we are looking for ways to occupy our minds with something is that we fear being left alone with our thoughts. But the attempt to run away doesn't really help for long, and only the light of presence can overcome the fear.

Meditation Won't Help If You Don't Understand This

Based on the exercises presented so far, you may conclude that presence is a kind of meditation, and though essentially it is, the concept is a bit different. For instance, a tiger won't practice meditation in an isolated room in order to catch its prey; it will concentrate on the actual mission. A child doesn't meditate when he pays his full attention to something he finds interesting; he (or she) is simply present.

Presence in the moment requires not only a practice routine. First and foremost, it requires the ability to watch our minds and understand the way fear-based thinking manifests in our lives.

Shaping Reality with Your Tongue

The way we enhance the fear and frustration created by fear-based thinking, is by speaking in the past and the future tenses, either aloud or within ourselves.

Reliving the past—"I should have done/said this and not that," "I wish I'd never met him," "She shouldn't have done this," "I've wasted time," "If only I knew," "If only it hadn't happened," or, "If only I had chosen differently."

Such statements express a refusal to accept the way things turned out, judgment, and remorse. Another, more constructive way of approaching a given situation, would be to ask yourself, "From what happened in the past, what can I learn for the future?" or, "What can I do now to achieve my goals?"

Enhancing fear of the future—"I'm afraid I won't persist," "I'm afraid of what others might think of me," "What if something happens?" "If that happens, it's not going to be that bad" (meaning, the worst-case scenario is about to happen and I'm trying to reassure myself it won't be that bad).

Every time we thoughtlessly use expressions such as "I'm

afraid" or "What if?" we increase our fear, and with our words we shape the reality we later experience. While it's natural to feel and express fear, the fears we express by projecting our thoughts into the future are related to imaginary scenarios that do not, and may never, exist.

Projecting the past into the future—"I won't be able to stand it again," "What if at the new job I'll feel the same as I felt at the old one?" "Why am I always like this?" (meaning, I was like this in the past and will be the same in the future), "I know exactly what she'll say!"

When we project the past into the future, we overlook the fact that our words and reactions can shape a future event. For instance, when we assume that we know how another person is going to react (even if based on his or her previous reactions), we approach him or her with certain expectations that are expressed in a certain tone: aggressive (due to the insult we already feel as a result of what we imagine will happen) or apologetic (for something that may not be a trouble at all). And sure enough, the approach we use draws the exact reaction we fear.

The Art of Listening to Your Thoughts

The art of listening to what's going on in our minds is the key to understanding why our reality looks the way it does, for better or worse.

When clients tell me they felt sad or angry for no apparent reason, I ask them, "What were you thinking about at the time?" "I didn't really think," they usually answer, and though they are not lying, they are mistaken, as we constantly think, except when we are temporarily distracted by something, barely conscious or asleep, or when we are fully present. Stress, anxiety, rage, and melancholy are most often the result of the thoughts that occupy our minds. Sometimes, however, we identify so deeply with the story behind the painful emotions that a slight reminder of the subject is enough to trigger the pain without needing to rethink the entire story.

Many, for example, consider their current life situation a direct outcome of their miserable childhood and not something they have a choice about. When they fall into melancholy, they don't have to think about those they hold accountable for their life circumstances and the things they have done. The story is always in the background and constantly affects the level of anger and despair they experience when something is not working out in the present moment.

Once you start listening to your thoughts, you will find that a significant portion of your internal monologue is occupied with complaining about the situation, about others, about what you missed, or about what might happen if you won't achieve your goals, with self-criticism, and with comparison to others in which you are frequently the underdog. When we start paying attention to our thoughts, we can quiet our minds by bringing our attention back to the present moment. Then, if possible, we can act with calmness and determination to change the situation.

As a first step, try to notice when you are speaking in the past or the future tense, out loud or within yourself. When you notice it, note to yourself, "I'm creating an imaginary scenario about the future again," or, "I'm caught in past stories again." By noticing the thought patterns while they happen, the identification with them starts to subside, and even if the unwanted thoughts won't disappear immediately, their grip will weaken and they will no longer have full control over your feelings.

Presence in Daily Life

Often, while we are physically in one place, our thoughts are somewhere else. Furthermore, we resist the situation we are in and the tasks we have to do. Instead, daily activities can be used as an opportunity to practice presence. Different activities require different levels of presence—some can be executed with minimal attention while others require our fullest attention. The quality of the task and our ability to enjoy it will be highly influenced by the alert, non-judgmental attention we pay to it.

Activities that require a high level of presence are reading, giving a lecture, acting, writing an essay, creative activities, and sports. Activities that are largely influenced by our level of presence are spending time with a child or an adult, listening to another person, the quality of our work, and making love. Activities such as spending time in nature enhance presence naturally, and most screen activities decrease our attention span and affect our ability to be present.

Presence as a Problem Solver

Often we're exhausting ourselves in an attempt to convince ourselves of different ideas or trying to deal with the challenges we face by making endless lists of pros and cons. Such thinking-based strategies, however, usually fail in providing a long-term, satisfying solution. It's presence, unexpectedly, that always leads to the best solution. Let's see how.

Perceiving Reality Through the Nightmares in Our Heads

The power of observation was given to humans so they would be able to understand the world, the animals, and the people around them. "Look around," God said. "Listen carefully," he added, "not to the words, as they will deceive you, but to what's behind them, to what's not being said: to a tone of voice, to a gap between the words, to a sigh, and to pain reflected through the eyes; to a dog's wagging tail or to its raised hackles."
~ From "The Five Wondrous Powers"

Due to the grip of fear-based thinking, most of the time we experience reality through our fears and our limiting beliefs. Instead of reacting directly to what's in front of us, we react to the "movies" in our heads. This failure of perception distorts the reality we are experiencing and creates intense pain. Below are some of the ways in which this distortion is manifested.

The feeling that everyone is judging me—Many, not only those who suffer from social anxiety, live in a constant feeling that everyone judges and mocks them. They feel uncomfortable even when walking down the street. In their minds there's an imaginary world that feeds off their feelings of worthlessness, and the judgment that reflects off other people's eyes is their judgment toward themselves.

Responding to our fears instead of the facts—A client who started dating someone new declares, "He probably thinks I'm boring."

"Do you think he would have bothered calling you every day for the last two weeks if that's what he thinks?" I ask.

Without presence she finds it hard to doubt her thoughts, which in her mind locks as real as the facts before her eyes.

Listening to the words instead of what is behind them—
Blinded by a distorted perception of reality and by empty words, we hardly ever try to sense the energy behind another person's words, and fail to look into his or her eyes to see what he or she really means. A child might reject his or her mother not because he or she doesn't want her affection, but because the child feels that the mother's affection is not genuine. When someone says to his or her spouse, "We better break up," he or she often means, "Please prove to me that you want me; please don't give up on me!"

All the information that we need is always in front of us, while we look for it in the chaos of our minds. When we say, "He tricked me," or, "Up to this moment I didn't realize who she is," it's because we didn't bother, or might have been afraid, to look behind the mask presented by the person. When I ask clients who are in a new relationship, "What did you learn about the person you are dating?" "Not much," they usually answer. They avoid asking the most burning questions and overlook the information in front of their eyes, as they fear it will taint the perfect image they created and force them to make unwanted decisions.

When presence grows within us, we slowly begin to hear what's beyond the words and the voices in our heads and to see clearly what is in front of us.

Breaking Free from the Majority of Our Problems

Most of our problems are nothing but imaginary scenarios full of fear of the future, such as, "What if the next time I meet someone, the same thing happens again?" "What if because of what he did to me I'll never trust anyone again?" "What will I do if I get fired?" or, "What if my money runs out?"

Nevertheless, we dedicate enormous energy to these thoughts, instead of focusing on productive actions that can help us achieve our goals. And according to our thoughts and actions, often our fears come true.

If our attention was rooted in the present moment, we would have noticed that what we foresee is not an inevitable future but only an unwanted scenario that is merely a thought.

Becoming a Naturally Positive Person

Different spiritual teachings that are based on the positive thinking genre emphasize mental and behavioral aspects essential to leading a happy and fulfilling life, including gratitude, acknowledging the abundance around us, releasing fear, and trusting the universe to bring us what we want. The way they recommend implementing these ideas is through techniques such as repeating positive affirmations, creating a list of the positive aspects of our lives, and expressing our belief in our ability to achieve the outcomes we desire.

To some extent, such techniques are beneficial. Their downside, however, is that they attempt to solve the problems created by the thinking mind with additional thinking—that is, an attempt to control our thoughts. Due to the enormous energy of fear-based thinking and the fact that most of us are only aware of a small portion of our thoughts, it's not possible.

When presence grows within us, those aspects become a natural part of our lives. We begin to notice the beauty around us and with it comes deep gratitude that requires no words, we begin to feel the good in our lives without needing to convince ourselves it is there, we feel much more comfortable with uncertainty, and less intimidated by challenges. And it just happens—with hardly an effort.

Finding Peace and Inner Strength

Sometimes we feel as if the ground dropped from beneath our feet. Old behavioral patterns reappear, fear takes control, and our emotions steam as if we are about to explode.

In an attempt to run away from our feelings, we try not to be alone or we use substances to numb our emotional pain. But while being left without distractions is what we fear most in such moments, being present and still is what can help us the most to find peace and inner strength.

Therefore, at times I feel I just want to run away from myself, I sit down on the couch and practice "five minutes of stillness."

Unlocking the Creativity of the Soul

When fear-based thinking starts to subside and we no longer identify with our thoughts, out of the peaceful place within us a new way of thinking arises—creative thinking. Suddenly new ideas and insights just flow, along with the realization, "I just know what to do!"

The Joy of Being

Presence completely changes the way we experience life. While social conventions push us to reach for as much as possible, presence invites us to experience the depth of life, so that even if on the surface not much is happening, the richness of each experience is beyond words.

It is not an exaggeration to say that before we learn to be present and experience the joy of being, we are not truly alive.

∴

In addition to the exercises presented in this chapter, there are many ways to make presence part of your life. I invite you to visit the "Guide to Practicing Presence" at the end of the book and to create your own ways of practice.

(Note that some of the exercises in the guide relate to insights presented further in the book, and thus will be fully understood after reading the entire book.)

PART THREE

Consciousness, Responsibility, and Choice

Chapter 6

Emotions: The Key to Success

There is a wide agreement that there's a general failure in the way the human species has been designed. This failure is responsible for the fact that many of us are still controlled by an emotional system that did not become extinct, as expected, at adulthood, and did not clear the way, as it was meant to, for rational thinking.

The ironic description above is sadly the common way most of us treat our emotions—as a flaw we should overcome. If we had the choice, most of us would like to keep enjoying emotions such as happiness, satisfaction, and joy, but everyone would agree that we should overcome "negative" emotions, or, more precisely, eradicate them.

Fear and reticence are often associated with experiencing and expressing emotions. Many children who experienced pain they didn't know how to deal with made an unconscious decision to repress their emotions as a defense mechanism, and as grown-ups they still fear the pain their feelings might create if acknowledged. Reticence to feel and express painful emotions is also an outcome of the way many of the adults in our lives expressed their emotions—through constant anger, rage outbursts, ugly arguments with each other, crying, or emotional dependence on us, their children.

Most children intuitively understand that what they witness is unhealthy and even destructive. When they look at the drama around them they often say to themselves, "I will never be like him/her." But as the nature of resistance is to strengthen what it opposes, often they find themselves acting in the exact way they condemn.

In the most important chapter of this book, I'm going to show you why your emotional system is not a flaw but the most powerful tool for a life of happiness and choice, why the way you normally express your emotions is destructive, and how to effectively use this magnificent tool you were given.

Why Are Your Emotions Making You Miserable?

The distinction between natural emotions and what I call "drama-based emotions" or "emotional drama" (from the word drama – a play) is the key to peace of mind, emotional stability, and happiness.

The emotional system is a sensory feedback mechanism that allows us, through the feelings that arise within us, to make beneficial choices and communicate effectively with others, just as physical sensations such as heat, cold, hunger, and satiety do. The emotional spectrum contains a range of emotions; those perceived as positive and those perceived as negative. All are natural and all have a role.

Drama-based emotions, unlike natural emotions, are not a direct response to circumstances but the result of a sad story that we build around them. The focus of the sad story is the self—its pain and satisfaction. The drama is enhanced by a dramatic interpretation added to the facts, appropriate intonation, and meaningful facial expressions. This is the exact same drama on which the most successful soap operas are based.

The following table emphasizes the differences between natural emotions and their drama-based counterparts.

Natural Emotions	Drama-Based Emotions
Fear	Anxiety
Fear is an instinctive reaction intended to maintain caution and keep the body alive.	Anxiety is a fruit of a sad and frightening scenario about future events that may never happen, or disproportionate reaction to a current event.
Envy	Jealousy
Envy is the feeling that lets us know what attracts us and what do we want for ourselves.	Jealousy is driven by the belief that another person's achievements are at my expense; that he or she will succeed more than I and make me feel inferior, or win something I own or desire.

Natural Emotions	Drama-Based Emotions
Disappointment	Bitterness and remorse
When we fail at something or don't achieve what we want, it's only natural to feel disappointment.	When thought interferes, we blame ourselves or lay the blame on the person whom we hold accountable for our disappointment, and as a result, we may experience feelings of bitterness and remorse over time.
Anger	Resentment, hatred, and grudges
Anger is an essential alert mechanism that notifies us when we hurt ourselves, when someone else hurts us, or when the current circumstances no longer suit us and require a change.	Resentment, hatred, and grudges are thought creatures that add a story to the feeling of anger. The essence of the story is that someone else should (and could) have behaved differently and therefore he or she is to blame. The story, which can be maintained for a lifetime, keeps the anger alive and amplifies it dozens of times. Hatred may also be the result of unrequited love—we use it to mentally avenge those who denied us their love and humiliated us.

Natural Emotions	Drama-Based Emotions
Hurt feelings	Rage, resentment, and hatred
Feeling hurt is a natural reaction to an emotional hit, the same way pain is to a physical one. Nevertheless, most people are swift to deny being hurt, as they perceive it as a shameful weakness.	Rage, resentment, and hatred mask hurt feelings, but unless we acknowledge the true feelings that lie beneath them, the pain will not dissolve.
Sadness and grief	Self-pity
Sadness and grief are natural reactions to events such as death, a breakup, or the end of a significant period in our lives.	In self-pity, the feeling of sadness is fueled by a sad story about what we believe we were owed and denied, by resentful thoughts about those whom we hold responsible for our life circumstances, by scary tales about the dark future that awaits us, and by inner resistance to *what is*.
Love	Obsessive love
Love is a powerful emotion—the essence of creation—that exists beyond needs and expectations.	Obsessive love (mainly romantic) is a sort of addiction developed around a good feeling provided by another person's admiration, and therefore, it easily causes huge emotional pain and drastic reactions when we dread losing it.

Natural Emotions	Drama-Based Emotions
Discomfort	Fear of rejection and failure
It's only natural that in certain situations or in front of new people we feel discomfort and find it hard to fully express ourselves.	Fear of rejection and failure (which some are quick to call social anxiety disorder) contains a strong motive of a self who judges him- or herself through the eyes of others and dreads judgment, rejection, and failure. "How will I look?" "What will people think of me?" "What if I am criticized or rejected?"
Natural guilt	Self-condemnation
Natural guilt is an essential guiding mechanism that directs us to treat fellow human beings, the earth, and all living things with consideration and respect.	Self-condemnation serves as a conceptual repair mechanism that says, "Though I did wrong, at least I'm aware of it and angry with myself for it." Often the expressed regret aims to show the distress of the offender and to push the one who feels hurt to forgive him or her. Inducing a guilt trip in another person is a way to manipulate him or her into doing what we want by causing feelings of guilt or fear of a possible unwanted outcome.

Natural Emotions	Drama-Based Emotions
Compassion	Pity
Compassion is the ability to feel other people's pain and care deeply for them without becoming part of their personal drama.	Pity has two aspects; one is the result of over-identification with another person's pain based on the thought of what we would have felt in his or her place. The other is a self-enhancement mechanism in which the so-called sympathy is intended to belittle the other person.
Joy and happiness	Craving for excitement
Joy and happiness are delightful feelings that arise when listening to a loved song, achieving something we wanted, anticipating a desirable experience, spending time with the people we love, fully expressing ourselves, being acknowledged by others, or for no specific reason.	Craving for excitement is the need to be constantly occupied with something that will save us from the emptiness within us. There's an addictive, fear-based, quality to it, as when the exciting event is over we are doomed to go back to the unwanted routine of our lives.
Aversion and repulsion	Contempt
Feelings of aversion or repulsion may sometimes arise in response to someone's energy.	Contempt satisfies the desire for superiority by demeaning another person, which can go as far as overlooking his or her humanity.

Natural emotions, when we don't resist them, evaporate in time and leave no residue. The identification with the sad story built around the circumstances keeps the drama-based emotions alive for a very long time, sometimes for a lifetime, and leaves behind a residue of emotional pain that permeates every aspect of our lives.

Emotional drama creates emotional chaos; it drives uncontrollable and obsessive behavior, creates stress and desperate pain, and as long as the need to alleviate the pain is burning, we find it hard to behave in a manner that supports our true goals and to respect the wishes and needs of others.

Crying, like any emotional reaction, might be an expression of natural or drama-based emotions. Crying that feeds off emotional drama may provide momentary relief, but at the same time its expression enhances the identification with the sad story that triggered it. The story—about how we've been wronged, our bad luck, and our hopeless future—which we express aloud or run in our heads, can make the crying go on for hours and days. Young children learn quickly to use dramatic crying to achieve what they want, and the parents who are swift to surrender to the pitiful and deafening screams teach them that it pays. Sometimes, however, a child's crying that seems disproportionate to the situation may be an expression of emotional pain that has accumulated due to the atmosphere at home and the attitude toward him or her. When the drama subsides, crying might still occur when grieving or remembering someone dear who is no longer with us, as a response to a touching book or movie, when compassion arises, or when we express suppressed pain. It will be quiet and fairly short, sometimes just tears filling the eyes.

The energetic frequency created by emotional drama

may be called "negativity." It doesn't mean that the person expressing it is inherently negative, but that by building and expressing it, emotional drama creates dense and painful energy within him. This energy affects his health, the way he experiences the world, and the nature of the people and events that come into his (or her) life.

The "Benefits" of Emotional Drama

Though emotional drama creates enormous pain, it conceals benefits as well, and as long as we keep using it, it means that unconsciously we believe that the benefits outweigh the pain. Let's examine some of the common ways we tend to use it.

Building a personal identity around painful events—A common belief is that in order to free ourselves from long-standing emotional pain we need to release its residue from the body or to thoroughly analyze everything that happened in the past. But despite the temporary relief such techniques provide, as long as we are not closely familiar with the thought patterns and ways of expression that breathe life into our old stories in the present moment, the pain will be kept alive and haunt us.

Statements such as, "I was traumatized," "I'm a victim of sexual abuse," "I suffer from anxiety" (when it is not an anxiety disorder), or, "My mother is toxic" intensify the pain and build an identity of a "victim" or a "sufferer" in the person expressing them. And why would anyone want to strengthen such an identity, you may ask. Because victimhood can gain us privileges, such as the privilege to hold grudges against the ones who hurt us and hurt them back, or the privilege to pity ourselves and, therefore, to allow ourselves to behave in an inconsiderate and disrespectful way to others.

A different, more fact-based description of the same circumstances immediately changes the emotions associated with them. "I was involved in a severe car accident," "I grew up in a very challenging home environment," "I was sexually molested," "I fear that ...," or, "My mother can be difficult. I must learn how to set clear boundaries with her."

Using self-pity as manipulation—Many learn to manipulate others by demonstrating sadness and helplessness. A child of protective parents may adopt this strategy at an early age, sometimes during infancy, as he quickly understands the gain it brings; he doesn't have to make an effort, and there will always be someone to take care of and do things for him. Although the child benefits from using this strategy, the problem is that he quickly forgets it's only a strategy. He learns to pity himself and to believe he cannot do things by himself. At adulthood, such a person keeps looking for someone to protect and look after him (or her), even in the most inadequate places such as workplaces or romantic relationships.

By using self-pity to manipulate others we're creating a paradox, because when people do things for us out of mercy—for instance, inviting us to hang out with them because they pity us for being alone—we feel frustrated. But since this behavioral pattern often provides immediate benefits, some fail to give it up despite the pain it creates.

Manipulation toward God for not giving me what I want—"If it won't happen I will commit suicide!" Have you ever heard this sentence? I'm sure you have. I've heard it more than once from women who faced difficulties finding a life partner, and I, too, years ago, when I was unemployed (for only four months), had thoughtlessly told my mother that if my money ran out and I'd have to come back home, I'd commit suicide. (I wasn't even close to running out of money before I found a new job. And anyway—I didn't have any intention to execute my threats). Nonetheless, the result of the unnecessary tension I created was severe hair loss I'd suffered after finding a new job.

Behind the exaggerated drama of such statements hides manipulation directed toward the world, or, more accurately, toward the creator of the world, that even though he sees my suffering, he won't give me what I want. Many who claim to be complete atheists use such manipulation.

Presenting the situation in a tendentious manner—Often we present the facts in a tendentious manner that justifies self-pity and blame, as demonstrated in the following statements. "The fact that he left me means he was playing me all along" (the assumption in the sentence is not a fact, but merely an interpretation); "I've wasted two years of my life on her" (those two years probably concealed good moments as well as significant learning in them. And even if not, crying over the past is nothing but a waste of precious time in the present moment); "I don't know if my mother loves me" (my mother doesn't love me the way I expect her to, so for all I care it's not love. And if you try to imply otherwise I will add to the story elements that support my argument).

Many believe that when they condemn the person who hurt them they pay this person back and lessen their yearning for him or her. But though mudslinging our current enemy satisfies a wounded ego for a moment, in doing so, we deliberately overlook the good times, create a victim-villain narrative, and as a result, we perceive our lives as painful and meaningless. A client who divorced her husband was not willing to acknowledge the good times they shared, although she admitted that it wasn't all bad. By doing so she felt she was balancing the pain he caused her. In practice, she was hurting herself by intensifying her anger and pain, and the turbulent emotions that blinded her pushed her to treat her ex-husband in a way that was hurting her children too.

Using illness to gain attention—The care and attention given to a sick person may turn sickness into a prize and create the temptation to misuse it. When I was nine I developed a "medical syndrome" of coughing attacks, when I found I could do it purposely. I did it because I was jealous of one of my classmates who suffered from asthma and wanted to be like her. I kept up this show for a few years, and as a result today I cough easily, and when I'm having a cold my deep and loud cough startles passers-by.

Due to the isolated structure of our society, often elderly people long for attention. Illness, unfortunately, is an easy way to attract it. For this reason, one may find himself inflating every symptom and talking about his medical condition incessantly, as if deriving pleasure from it. He claims he wants to feel better, but in a way, having to deal with his medical condition relieves the burden of his (or her) emotions.

∴

Emotional drama has an addictive nature, and when we learn to believe the drama we've created, we become tremendously miserable. Sometimes, when the pain becomes unbearable, we realize that we can't go on this way and we start to awaken.

Acknowledging the Underlying Emotion to Heal the Pain

Denial of unwanted emotions is a social norm. Often, after a breakup, people try to encourage their heartbroken friends by saying, "You shouldn't feel this way," "Just don't think about it," "There's no point in being angry," or, "Okay, next!" Parents, in an attempt to protect their children, sometimes say unrealistic things like, "Jealousy is a word that has no place in our home." Such statements are so commonly accepted that we don't need to hear them in order to be ashamed of our feelings and deny their existence.

Those who suppress their feelings are perceived as strong. Men, especially, are "forbidden" to show emotions lest they be perceived as feminine and weak. People are so used to deny their true feelings, that often when you ask someone, "What do you feel?" he or she looks at you with a slight shock and starts the answer with the words "I think…."

But suppressed emotions won't dissolve; they burn inside us like a toxic acid, affect the body and the soul, and eventually explode at the least appropriate moment.

The Effective Way to Acknowledge Emotions

The effective way to acknowledge emotions begins with giving up their denial. For this purpose, we have to learn to identify the multiple strategies that are commonly used to cover unwanted feelings.

Positive slogans—Statements such as, "It's all for the best," "I have no expectations," "Everything happens for a reason," or, "Something better is waiting for me," despite the truth concealed in them, at the moment of truth, when our emotions still burn inside, are a lie, a slogan we repeat. Even someone who understands that everything that happens is really for the best, still feels pain in the face of unwanted circumstances. Statements such as, "I choose to see the glass as half full," as well, are often a lip service that hides the fear to acknowledge what's missing.

Rational decisions—Rational decisions, such as, "I changed my attitude," or, "I decided not to care anymore," sound like a good idea. However, when rational understanding takes place before the underlying emotions have been acknowledged, it does more harm than good. For instance, an adult who understood that his parents did the best they could and, therefore, there is no reason for him to be angry with them, will keep feeling irrational anger as long as he holds them accountable for his condition. Such a person might add to his pain by judging himself for not being able to implement the rational decision he (or she) made.

Accepting the situation in good spirits—When I hear statements such as, "I decided to laugh about it instead of getting angry," I wonder how our friends in the animal kingdom would manage if they held back their instinctive reactions and gave up their boundaries. Indeed, some things are not worthy of our anger, but sometimes we need to make it clear that someone has violated our boundaries. It's not funny when someone is laughing at my expense, or when someone curses and hoots violently and floods my environment with negative energy when I'm sitting with him or her in the car.

Suppressing our inner voice—When someone says, "I don't know what I feel," he or she is actually saying, "What I believe I should want or feel doesn't reconcile with what I'm really feeling, and I'm not willing to accept my emotions."

Denying "inadequate" feelings—Denial of certain emotions that are perceived as a weakness, such as anger, jealousy, being hurt, or longing for someone who hurt us, is a common practice.

A client whose friend got into a new relationship told me about it and immediately added, "Of course I feel happy for her." Yet her facial expression and tone of voice testified otherwise. She was trying to suppress her natural envy and the feeling of loss that naturally arises when we fear that someone close might drift away. "I don't want to be such a person that can't be happy for others," she added. But whether admitting it or not, she is "such a person"—only human, like the rest of us.

Condemning ourselves for the way we feel—If you listen to yourself, as well as to other adults, you will probably find yourself apologizing or condemning yourself for the way you feel. "It's stupid," "I shouldn't feel this way," "I should have already gotten over it by now," "What nonsense am I dealing with while others are sick or starving," or, "In a perfect world I wouldn't care about it."

A young woman whose mother constantly commented on her clothing and hair was judging herself harshly for letting it bother her. Her inner voice, expressed by her anger, insisted that something was wrong, but instead of dealing with the cause of her anger—her mother's interference in her personal affairs—she made herself feel like a failure for being influenced by her mother's words.

Verbal contradictions—Often people instinctively express what they really feel. "It annoys me!" "I still miss her," or, "The thought that I'll never meet someone like him is painful."

Then, when hearing themselves, they are quick to deny what they perceive as a weakness by contradicting what they just said. "I don't really care," "It's not that I think about her daily," or, "Even if I could I wouldn't want to be with him."

Replacing one emotional addiction with another—A common way of dealing with painful emotions is the attempt, which often succeeds, to shift the focus of our emotions toward a new object. After a breakup many try to ease the pain through a new relationship; a grudge against the mother dissolves when replaced with a new one, against the husband; and a relationship that provides a false sense of love eases our loneliness and pain for a while.

Despite the immediate relief it provides, replacing one emotional addiction with another cannot solve the root problem, and the emotions we have run from will sooner or later reappear.

A healthy and beneficial way to acknowledge our feelings is to simply describe them without resistance ("I don't understand why I feel this way") or drama ("It's terrible," "It shouldn't have happened," "I failed again; something is fundamentally wrong with me!").

Often, all you need in order to release an emotional burden is to simply admit your true feelings by saying something like, "Yes, I am jealous," the same way a child says, "I want ice cream too!" to simply express what you really feel: "I still love him even though he left me," "I'm hurt," or, "I'm angry." The more the topic is meaningful to you, the longer it might take to let go of the pain, though you will probably feel immediate relief when you stop judging yourself for the way you feel.

The fear of acknowledging our true feelings has far-reaching consequences: painful emotions that won't let go for years; grudges that flare up over and over again between partners, friends, and relatives; and health effects including life-threatening diseases. But the person who hasn't awakened yet considers admitting his true feelings far more intimidating. He will cling to the image he built, lie, deny, and suppress his emotions; he would rather pay a heavy price than acknowledge the truth. It would be pointless to try to convince him (or her) to act otherwise.

Acknowledging Another Person's Feelings

Difficulty, or, more accurately, unwillingness to acknowledge other people's feelings, is the source of the feeling that "my situation is the worst" and a justification for self-pity. The willingness to acknowledge the feelings of those around us stems from the understanding that there is no correlation between external circumstances and inner state, and that even if someone has exactly what we want, he or she may experience difficulty and pain.

A couple is seeking my help due to constant arguments. "Sometimes I'm really mad at him for saying he's facing difficulties; it's not that he's been through what I have," the woman says. And, indeed, she suffered a lot of pain, but so did he, pain that drove him to depression. From her point of view, though, his life circumstances do not justify the pain and, therefore, she is not willing to accept his feelings as legitimate.

Often we judge other people's feelings from our point of view and dismiss them out of hand ("What right do you have to be angry?"). Instead of trying to understand why they are sad or withdrawn, we are quick to assume that their mood reflects something we did, and instead of considering their feelings, we demand that they soothe ours.

When the argument gets heated and both sides lay the blame on each other, often what they really want is for their partner to acknowledge their feelings. They keep attacking and justifying themselves desperately hoping to hear something like, "I'm sorry for hurting you," even if from the other person's point of view they had no reason to be offended.

Identifying Your Pain-Colored Glasses

Sometimes it's not that we deny our feelings but that we are unaware of their true cause. The pain within us creates a kind of glasses through which we perceive the world. Each of us wears slightly different glasses, depending on the experiences that shaped his or her pain, which can be identified through the statements someone automatically repeats when describing different relationships in his or her life, such as, "People don't like me," "I'm always being rejected," "Everyone acts like I'm invisible," or, "People always lie to me/humiliate me." Due to this perception we are constantly on the lookout, expecting the hurtful attitude we are familiar with, and easily interpreting an innocent comment as an insult.

I, for example, used to react aggressively when I thought my colleagues did not respect me. I perceived the men in my life as weak and just waited for the moment they would fail me, and my belief that people, in general, find it hard to accept me led me to judge them and avoid their company. There's no doubt I haven't seen the world clearly.

Only when we learn to identify our pain-colored glasses, we find how distorted the reality reflected through them was.

Is Your Anger Normal?

If you want to know whether a certain behavior or emotion is natural, look at young children or animals. One of the emotions many think is wrong, and, therefore, are afraid to feel and express, is anger.

"Me? I rarely get angry," is a sentence I often heard when working as an HR recruiter. You can only imagine how jealous I was of those serene people. But already then, despite believing them, I had some doubts, and, therefore, I would add, "And what would your wife/husband say about it?" Then, as expected, their reaction would change.

A child naturally reacts with anger when he doesn't get what he wants, when he fails at something, when an adult interrupts his play, or when he envies his (or her) baby brother or sister. Children are not afraid to express anger but they don't hold grudges; they express their emotions and then move on.

Anger is a natural emotion, and like all emotions, it has a purpose. The purpose of anger is to indicate what is right and what is wrong for us, when people overstep our boundaries, or when we are mistreating ourselves.

Spiritual seekers often hold on to the unrealistic image of the "good and full of love person" who never feels anger. Holy Scripture commentary supports the assumption that anger is wrong by calling it a bad measure, and parents implant the idea that anger is wrong by saying things like, "There's no need to get angry!" Anger, however, is not a mistake or a bad measure, and the way to overcome it is not by trying to convince ourselves that we have no reason to be angry, but by changing the aspects that create it.

The social suppression of anger is an instrument in the

hands of those who have an interest in manipulating others in order to gain money and power, as it's easy to manipulate someone who doesn't respect his feelings, doesn't listen to the feedback they supply, and judges himself harshly for the way he (or she) feels.

The Fear of Anger

I can easily understand why people are so afraid of their anger. Before I awakened I was full of anger; my anger was sabotaging every aspect of my life—my relationships with my family, friends, and colleagues. It made me lose control and then feel guilty and ashamed of myself.

Some fear anger because they have witnessed their parents expressing it in a destructive way. As a result, they have adopted the opposite behavior—from the outside they seem gentle and serene, while the burning emotions inside them are directed mainly toward themselves and a few close relatives.

Often people say, "If I allow myself to be angry, I'm afraid I will lose control." But despite their attempts to hold back the anger, at some point they explode, unable to control themselves. Ironically, their actions lead to the exact thing they were trying to avoid. Only when they learn to acknowledge their anger, respect it, and, when needed, express it without drama, will the emotional outbursts cease.

Aggression versus Firmness

Due to the fear of feeling and expressing anger, often when we want to say, "No," or, "That's it!" we keep smiling and say, "Okay," and, "No problem." The difficulty of maintaining our boundaries and respecting ourselves arises mainly in front of those we perceive as superior to us or whose reaction we fear.

Many parents, for example, are reluctant to be firm with their children, either because they think it's wrong or because they are afraid that their children will stop loving them. But those parents who are so afraid not to please their children, eventually find themselves lashing out at them.

Firmness can be used as a message that aims to set boundaries and declare, before anger shows up, "That's it!" or, "I'm the one in charge here," exactly as animals do in order to clarify to their enemies, "This is my territory," and avoid a needless fight.

Children, as well as adults, respond negatively to disrespectful behavior. When treated fairly and respectfully, even if firmly, they may express dissatisfaction but their anger will soon dissipate.

Anger as Manipulation

We learn to use anger at a young age simply because it gets us results. When a child screams and his mother gives in, he learns to use anger to his advantage, but soon he learns to believe the drama he (or she) has created as well. Thus, as adults we may lack control over our emotions and may easily be drawn into dramatic expressions of anger that involve shouting and crying.

Another common manipulation is what's called "cold shoulder"—when we wear an angry face so that the other person will understand his or her mistake and make an attempt to please us.

The problem with these tactics is that manipulations amplify our anger and sense of victimhood, and the moment we use them, the drama we've created becomes a solid reality for us.

Anger That We Feel When Someone Pities Us

When someone pities us, it makes us feel weak, be ashamed of ourselves, and hide from this person so that he or she won't witness our faults.

When a mother, for instance, pities her unmarried daughter and treats her as someone who deserves special care, perhaps she believes that her concern reflects love and care. In practice, she only lays the burden of her emotions on her daughter's shoulders and makes her feel even worse.

Though a young child who is being pitied cannot do anything about it, as adults we have full control over it, as the world is like a giant mirror—and, therefore, once we no longer pity ourselves, no one can pity us. If you don't believe me, just try it.

Anger as a Reminder

One of my clients couldn't let go of anger toward a healer who treated her. She held him accountable for failing to supply the promised cure for a medical condition she suffered from, though along the course of the treatment her inner voice had warned her over and over again that something was wrong. I had a hard time letting go of anger toward a consultant I used to see. I resented him for not taking responsibility for the fact that our meetings had become counterproductive, despite knowing that I kept seeing him because I enjoyed his company.

Anger, in situations like these, is simply a reminder that says, "I don't ever want to find myself in such a situation again." Blame, on the other hand, overlooks our responsibility for the situation by holding someone else accountable.

Without blame, the feeling of anger may persist as long as we need the reminder it provides. It helps us understand what path we don't want to take again and how we can manage similar situations better in the future.

Anger Resulting from Self-Disrespect

Self-disrespect is a lack of honoring one's own wishes and needs. Women, for example, often find themselves bearing an unequal share of the household chores. Sometimes, due to the culture they were raised in, they don't even admit to themselves that it bothers them. But even when they manage to justify the situation, their souls protest with anger.

A fundamental form of self-disrespect is having a relationship with someone who is emotionally unavailable, unwilling to commit, or married. Many who find themselves in such situations cling to a range of excuses in order to justify their choices. "It's better than nothing," "Sex is a basic human need," "I don't have feelings for her," "It's exactly what suits me right now," or, "If we were together, he would only make me miserable." But despite the seed of truth in their words, the sense of humiliation inherent in such relationships is so profound that no excuse can erase it. Sometimes, above all justifications, only the anger keeps protesting.

Often self-disrespect takes place at seemingly insignificant moments that can easily be ignored; when we let others mistreat us and pretend that everything is okay, or when we do something for someone else, not because he or she cannot do it for him- or herself but because he or she complains it's too hard.

Sometimes someone constantly makes us angry. In such situations, many tend to automatically blame themselves for getting angry, instead of trying to figure out what behavior of this person triggers their anger. And when others invalidate their feelings ("What is it with you?" "Why are you getting angry?" "What's the problem with what he said?"), they are quick to agree that their judgment is wrong.

Self-betrayal is another form of self-disrespect. It happens with our parents when we act upon their expectations instead of upon our wishes, with our children when we give in to their nagging in order to win another moment of peace, with friends whom we are afraid to lose if we say what bothers us, when we agree to physical intimacy against our will, when we try to behave in what we perceive as the right way against our inner guidance, or when we take on one too many tasks at work. Often we justify our decisions by statements such as, "This is how a good friend behaves," "You can't think only of yourself," "What can I do?" or, "There are some things you must do." Self-betrayal might be the result of an attempt to preserve an image of a good person at all costs, of compromising our standards for money or for momentary satisfaction, or an expression of fear. When it happens we feel as if something inside us squeaks. "Squeak, squeak, something here is wrong," our inner voice whispers, "Wanting to get married but giving permission to undefined relationships ... giving in to my child again ... meeting a friend though I really need some rest ... keeping a client I know I shouldn't keep only for his money." "Squeak, squeak," the voice tries again, and we keep ignoring it.

At the moment of betrayal, it's as if we've painted a large X on ourselves; "Insignificant! Worthy of nothing!" we've marked ourselves and lost all our strength in an instant. The uncontrollable chain of events that occurred afterward, like we were a brakeless train running down the hill, was a direct outcome of that moment.

Anger Toward Those Who Take Advantage of Us

Fear, pain, and feelings of worthlessness often drive humans to take advantage of their brothers to satisfy their own needs and run away from pain. Thus, if someone allows him- or herself to be exploited, there will always be someone that takes advantage of him or her.

Due to their need for protection and care, children cannot prevent abusive, manipulative, unfair, and disrespectful behavior toward them. But many adults behave as if they still don't have a choice, and thus adopt the victim identity. They keep knocking their heads against the wall for years, expecting something that will never happen. They fight, blame, and resent those who don't understand them and don't pay proper attention to their feelings and needs, instead of accepting that they can only change themselves and step away from the victim stance.

Anger About the Truth That Lies Beneath the Surface

Some are able, from a young age, to easily identify the truth behind the masks almost everyone wears. Like the child in the story "The Emperor's New Clothes" who calls out, "The king is naked!" they cannot deny the truth that lies beneath the nice words and the smiles.

Often they feel an instinctive aversion to a seemingly pleasant person, but since everyone else sees only the mask this person wears, they tend to doubt their instincts and judge themselves for feeling this way.

Holding on to Anger

In spite of the fear to feel and express anger, it seems that many people do carry and express a lot of anger. Anger that lasts for long, that accumulates and burns, must be based on resentment, hatred and blame—on a sad story that can be nurtured for years as if it was a monstrous pet. In such situations, the anger serves as a distraction from the things we'd rather not think about and supplies a false sense of power and superiority.

How Can You Control Your Emotions?

Despite the importance of acknowledging our emotions and expressing them in a healthy way, it's equally important to have a choice about the way we express them, so that they won't sabotage our relationships and stand in the way of our goals, and to regulate our emotions so that they won't overpower us. Think about someone who has inspired you—was it a "robot" who doesn't give him- or herself permission to feel anything? Or maybe a "drama queen" who seems as if he or she can't control his or her reactions? I guess not. It was most likely someone who has integrity, inner strength, the ability to feel and express love and to react to situations in a sensible way. And though it's not common, when we face someone like this, whether in reality, in a book, or in a movie, it touches our souls and inspires us to be at our best.

Emotions cannot be controlled by a rational decision, and anyone who's made the decision, "Tomorrow I'm starting a new chapter in my life," at least once, already knows that. Still, it is possible to achieve emotional balance and stability, so that even when we have to deal with difficult emotions, we are not overwhelmed by them.

Achieving emotional balance and having a choice about the way we feel and react to situations require giving up the emotional expressions that create the energy I called "negativity," and this might be challenging, as those expressions have become an integral part of our daily lives.

The Line Between Control and Lack of Control

At the moment of truth we have a choice: to enjoy the momentary satisfaction supplied by creating a drama around the circumstances, or to give it up when no one guarantees us alternative satisfaction.

Choosing the momentary satisfaction is choosing to "allow myself." "Allow what?" you may ask. To pity myself, talk ugly, act in an inconsiderate way due to my misery, say things that are meant to hurt, blame others while presenting myself as an innocent victim to anyone who would listen, or use sadness to draw attention and care—all those actions that provide an immediate sense of relief but at a cost: the intensification of the negative energy within us.

The negative energy we have built won't fade away when the drama is over. It keeps living inside us like an infection, painting everything black, creating anger, frustration, and burning pain—and as a result, a lack of control over our feelings and reactions.

"I Just Can't Accept That!" Is That True?

A major cause of unhappiness is the refusal to mentally accept *what is*, as reflected by the following statements. "I don't believe he doesn't love me," I can't accept that," "It shouldn't have happened," "How could she have done this?" or, "How come he doesn't understand?"

When we are arguing with *what is*, we are wasting essential time and energy and filling ourselves with deep frustration. But no matter how much we object, get angry, and insist on understanding something that cannot be explained, irreversible facts won't change.

At any given moment we can choose to cooperate with our life circumstances instead of denying the fact of their existence. As long as we dwell on what could or should have been, we are missing what's possible for us now. Accepting the "no" of our ex-partner is the first step toward the one who will say "yes" to us; the most important support the daughter can offer her sick father is to accept the fact of his illness without drama; and true intimacy in a relationship can be established only when we give up the demand that the other person change.

The Relationship Between Inner Acceptance and Inner Peace

The norm these days is to constantly complain about the circumstances and to express our frustration at what we have to do. "Why me?" "I can't stand it anymore," "I only did it for him," "I don't want to but I have to," we complain and keep doing the things we complain about. "I wholeheartedly chose to help my mother," says a client, "but…" she adds and contradicts herself, as the word "but" contradicts the meaning of the words that came before it.

When we act from a place of inner resistance, we create more harm than good. The unwillingness that accompanies our actions is felt on the other side, even if unconsciously, and makes the supported person feel as if we are doing him or her a favor out of mercy. Such an action also increases our frustration and sense of victimhood, and thus often leads to unnecessary outbursts of anger that wouldn't have happened if we respected our initial resistance.

Sometimes we can bring inner acceptance to a given situation simply by changing our attitude; at other times further action is required, as the following story demonstrates. My client was repeatedly frustrated by the behavior of her mother. When we discussed it, she understood that her judgmental attitude toward her mother was constantly making her angry, and thus affecting her quality of life. The next time we met she told me how she listened patiently to her mother's complaints for a long while. But it was clear that she acted in the way she believed was right and wasn't true to herself.

Inner resistance may naturally arise when listening to incessant complaints, as a message that says, "Enough! I don't want to fill myself with this energy." Such a feeling can support the relationship if I use it as a sign that it's time to say to my mother, "Let's drop this subject as there's nothing we can do about it," or to change the subject of the conversation before I get angry and make her feel foolish and judged. Instead, blaming my mother for her behavior by saying something such as, "No matter how many times I ask her, she just can't stop complaining," and judging her for her unconsciousness is what creates lasting anger and frustration.

We can't always enjoy everything we do, but in order to stop filling ourselves with useless negativity, we can bring inner acceptance to any action we choose to take, and to any situation in which we choose to remain. Then, if possible, we can focus on changing what's required instead of just complaining about it.

The Effects of Negative Motivation

Our meeting begins and my client looks at me with worry. "Last week I told you how good it felt to practice presence, but all of a sudden I realized there's a problem with it." As we continue our conversation, I understand that in her mind calmness is associated with indifference, and thus she believes that not being stressed about something is giving up on trying to achieve it.

Like many of us, she learned to believe that dissatisfaction, fear, and negativity are proper motives for change, an idea that drives a large part of the population to believe that if they accept the situation or, God forbid, enjoy it, they will remain stuck in the same place forever. Instead of pursuing their goals out of will, enjoyment, and creativity, they waste most of their lives waiting for the next achievement that will finally make them whole. Resisting their life situations doesn't help in any way; it only brings them more of what they focus on (what they don't want) and increases their pain.

The Cost of Your "Justified" Grudges

Among the drama-based emotions, grudges are the most intense and, therefore, have the most negative impact on our wellbeing. A grudge develops when we harbor negative feelings toward someone we believe has wronged us or someone dear to us, or when we hold others accountable for our life circumstances.

Our grudges may seem to us justified and even inevitable, because most often they are the result of hurtful, offensive, and abusive actions. But the main reason we carry such feelings for years, sometimes for a lifetime, is not the pain we have suffered. The pain would have dissolved after a while had it not been for the idea that what happened shouldn't have.

When we bear a grudge against another person, our accusations serve as proof that we are better than him or her. The sense of superiority gained by bearing a grudge is what makes it so hard to give it up, despite the enormous pain it creates.

The ability to forgive, to which many aspire, is nothing but letting go of the idea that someone is to blame. Because although hurtful things have been done, by blaming others for their actions we imply that they could have acted differently. Yet people can only act from their level of consciousness, and no treatment has ever helped someone who cannot help him- or herself.

It's often said that it's hard to forgive, that it requires nobility, that you can forgive but not forget—such statements provide us with justification to hold on to our grudges. When someone says, "I forgive him as I can only pity him," it's yet another form of self-enhancement gained by emphasizing the inferiority of another person.

In order to let go of your grudges, that is to say, to really forgive, you should learn to identify them also when they hide beneath seemingly innocent and justified statements. When someone says, "I'm not angry; I'm disappointed," his words conceal accusations. The sentence "They owe me that" is a score-settling with those who didn't pay back in the same coin. And a statement such as "I don't care anymore; he is dead to me" is something you wouldn't bother saying about someone you feel nothing for.

It's important to understand that forgiveness does not require action. When you forgive someone it's first and foremost for yourself; you may choose not to be in touch with the person whom you have forgiven or to maintain only a minimal level of contact. Sometimes it will be someone you can't or don't want to stay away from—in such a situation it would be wise to set clear boundaries to prevent further harm.

After giving up your grudges, natural anger may persist for a while, and from time to time you may still find yourself dwelling on the wrongs done to you. But when you no longer identify with your thoughts, they will ultimately lose their grip and subside.

Other than the immediate pain they create in the form of annihilating anger, a sense of melancholy, and lack of energy, in the long term resentment and grudges cause physical pain, chronic and fatal diseases, influence anxiety and depression, and might drive their owner to a behavior that can be perceived as "insane"—emotional outbursts, delusional thoughts, and aggressive actions that are driven by a thirst for revenge.

But despite the price we pay, the feeling derived from bearing a grudge is like a drug, and when we get addicted to it we need another "dose" each time. Just like drugs, the act of condemning others and throwing blame around supplies a sudden burst of power, and just like drugs, it leaves behind a residue of pain and destruction that requires another "dose" to mask it. Therefore, in order to let go of your grudges you need to truly want it, and be ready not only to give up the pain they create but also the sense of power and superiority they supply.

Self-Pity and the Saddest Story Competition

When asked if they pity themselves, few are those who are not quick to deny it, though the protest in their voices might imply otherwise. With the question, "Do you feel sorry for what happened to you?" (i.e., sorry for yourself), they are keener to agree. "Yes, it's sad," most of them answer. However, the sadness and the pain for what happened cannot live for months and years after the end of the event without help. They are kept alive as long as we hold others accountable for what happened to us and mourn what we had to endure.

The hasty use of the word "sadness" allows us to feel sorry for ourselves without admitting it. "I had a sad weekend," I often hear from my single clients. "Could it be more accurate to say that you felt sorry for yourself over the weekend?" I suggest. I know it's difficult to grasp before actually trying it—but when we give up self-pity, most of the sadness disappears, and the path toward fulfilling our wishes opens.

Other forms of self-pity are the harsh and unfair judgment we inflict on ourselves (consisting of repeated complaints about the way we feel, how we behaved, or what we desire); resistance to *what is* ("How the hell did I end up here?"); unwillingness to acknowledge our strength, to attribute our success to ourselves, or to see the good in our lives; and futile tears about an imaginary future scenario filled with sorrow ("It will never happen!").

To say that self-pity provides pleasure seems mistaken,

but it does have an addictive quality; the "addicts" indeed feel deep pain when the sad thoughts flood their minds, but the pain is spiced with a sweet expectation that someone will eventually witness their pain and set them free from their misery, as amusingly described by Curtis Sittenfeld in her book *Prep*.[3] "As a freshman, I had at times believed that if my sadness were intense enough, it would magnetically draw a handsome boy to my room to comfort me, and that had served as an incentive, when alone, to lie around and weep. But nothing had ever come of my exertions, and I'd finally realized that times passed faster if you were doing something, like watching TV or reading a magazine."

It's not that I'm underestimating the pain. Many these days experience a painful childhood; at a young age they have to deal with physical or verbal abuse, emotionally absent parents, scarcity, and loss. Even those whose circumstances seem favorable on the surface may experience huge pain. That's a fact. Often, however, when I listen to my clients, not only is their story revealed to me but also their need to be acknowledged as the ones who suffered the most.

At the beginning of my coaching career I had an eye-opening moment—one of my first clients was referred to me by a friend. When I spoke with my friend about my career aspirations, I told her, "I want to work with people who have faced difficult challenges in their lives, like your friend." She kept quiet for a moment. "Faced difficult challenges?" she asked. "Yes, she faced challenges in her life," she added, "but so have I, though I don't bother to mention it at every opportunity. And look how much she has today, yet she's never happy." At that moment I understood that when I buy into the sad story of my client, instead of helping her to let go of the past, my pity for her increases her self-pity. I also recalled how the exact same thing was said to me a few years earlier (that no matter what happens I'm never satisfied), and how already then, instead of being offended, I was stunned by this realization.

The thought that nourishes the sad story is that if certain things hadn't happened, everything could have been different for us. It's not past events, however, but the belief that they shouldn't have happened that keeps us from living our lives to the fullest in the present moment. Oprah Winfrey's story is an inspiring example. She was raised by her grandmother, who used to beat her and then expected her to act as if nothing had happened. For a few years, from childhood through adolescence, she was sexually molested by a relative, and because she desperately yearned for love, she allowed it. For years later, she blamed herself for what happened and buried her pain in food. Despite that and despite being an African American woman, she gained huge success, she is an inspiration for millions around the world, and "worthy of pity" is the last thing someone would think of her. When I watched an episode of her show, in which she interviewed sex offenders, just like the one who hurt her, I was astounded; when she spoke to them she expressed no anger, and when she described what she'd been through, there wasn't a shred of self-pity in her voice.

When we let go of self-pity, painful circumstances will not dissolve as if they never happened, but the feelings associated with them will significantly change. The major part of what I have been through seems to me now as an old story and no emotion is associated with it anymore. Sometimes I may regret the past—but what I regret is not my personal circumstances but not spending more time with those I love who are no longer with me or accepting their weaknesses with greater compassion.

The Mysterious Switch That Will Help You Give Up Your Negativity

Despite all that's been said, what seems the hardest when we deal with painful events or unwanted circumstances is giving up complaining, blaming, inner resistance, and most of all, self-pity.

A few years ago, I participated in a nine-month leadership program of the Coaches Training Institute (CTI). It was the most powerful experience I've ever had. And though a year earlier, when going through CTI's coaching training, I'd become a calmer and more peaceful person, during the leadership program old feelings suddenly appeared and again I felt different, unloved, judgmental, and angry. The third retreat of the program began with a day of silence. During this day I was preoccupied with my resentment toward two people; with one I'd just had an argument; from the other I'd experienced disappointment. As I didn't talk and didn't express my feelings otherwise, no one, allegedly, could have known my state of mind.

At dinner, an hour before the end of the silence day, I was sitting near one of the program's leaders, who mentioned earlier her sensitivity to energies. In the middle of the meal she suddenly got up and moved to another place. The voice in my head went wild. "She doesn't like me," I thought. "She can't stand my presence." My anger became stronger, and so did my self-pity. "No one likes me. People don't accept me and can't stand my company."

I finished my meal and sat down wallowing in anger and self-pity, when suddenly I realized that I was emitting the negative energy within me even when I didn't say a word, making the atmosphere around me unpleasant and uninviting. "Okay, I can keep pitying myself and be angry," I said to myself, "or I can give it up and become more inviting." And once I made this decision something within me changed; I felt lighter, and the things I complained about lost their significance.

To this day I'm not sure this was the reason the program's leader changed her seat, but it doesn't really matter. What matters is that as of this day I live in choice—the choice not to add drama and negativity to a given situation, as I understand the influence it has on my life and on the way people react to me.

The mysterious inner switch I discovered in a moment of despair is something each of us has, and activating it requires only the power of will; it's as if we are standing in front of a mighty wall, and suddenly it disappears just because we want it to. The wall is an imaginary wall inside us, and until the shift happens within us it seems impregnable. Then, in an instant it's gone and our entire reality changes.

Negativity's Battle for Survival

Even after the glorious awakening and the astonishing discovery of the inner switch, you have to understand the powers inside and around you that oppose the change and expect the sabotaging voice to keep whispering in your ears. "They did you wrong ... they hurt you," it will justify your sense of victimhood, encourage resentment and vindictiveness ("Don't be a sucker!"), and you will find it hard not to believe it.

You will find yourself drowning in a sea of melancholy and thinking, "But how will I not pity myself? How?" or, "What's wrong with feeling sorry for myself for a little while?" and justifying it with, "It's better to give yourself permission to feel than to suppress your emotions." You will emphasize the negative, disregard the positive, and refuse to see the situation in any other way. Only one thing will satisfy you—that all your wishes will be answered straightaway.

And though self-pity and blame don't make you a bad person, they take their toll—the blame you lay on others creates hard feelings that eat you up inside, and the energy created by self-pity is like a quagmire that lets you move only in one direction. Thus, if you choose not to give them up, at least do it consciously and not like a helpless victim.

The armor-bearers of fear don't want you to give up negativity. They want you to waste your energy in futile thoughts and useless actions that lead you nowhere. After all, if you weren't so desperate, how could they promise you salvation?

So if for a moment it looks like you have "stepped back" and all your achievements are gone, remind yourself that it's only fear trying to tighten its grip, and don't forget that presence is the key to break free from it.

Effortless Self-Love

After giving negativity up, one day, for no particular reason, an amazing thing happens—suddenly a big love arises, and instead of beating myself up for my failures and faults or dwelling on "what if?" like I used to, I find myself thinking of how satisfied I am with myself, recalling moments of power and joy, funny moments, fulfilling times with family and friends, thinking about people I love—and just feeling grateful for my life.

These are real positive thinking and self-love—they are not an outcome of tedious efforts to think positively, repeating affirmations, or going through programs that promise to build self-esteem; instead, they arise naturally by giving up drama and negativity.

From Fear to Love

You create your reality through your beliefs and your emotional energy. You create it out of fear or out of love. Fear creates lack of control; love enables the freedom of choice.

All emotions are a by-product of either love or fear. The source of all drama-based emotions is fear. Grudges mask feelings of worthlessness, blaming others provides a respite from blaming ourselves, jealousy stems from the belief that there is not enough for everyone, pity toward someone else creates a sense of superiority, and intense thrill doesn't leave room for thinking about the things that frighten us. The source of all natural emotion, even those considered negative, is love. Natural anger directs us to respect our preferences and needs, envy comes from the passion to live our lives to the fullest, disappointment is the result of unfulfilled desire that declares, "I'm still here!" Compassion, happiness, and aliveness are direct expressions of love.

Natural fear protects the body and keeps us away from danger. But the congenital sense of fear cannot guide us effectively through the veil of fearful thoughts that constantly occupy our minds, creating confusion, stress, and anxiety.

As the ruling energy of our culture, fear has a crucial influence on the choices each of us makes every day. The challenge of mankind, as individuals and as a collective, is to go beyond fear, toward love.

The Beliefs That Perpetuate the Collective Fear of Mankind

Two fundamental beliefs that enjoy broad consent keep us in the grip of fear.

1. The belief that there is not enough—time, money, suitable life partners, natural resources, land, or love.

This belief is the source of all wars between individuals and nations, of violence, oppression, and manipulation, of holding desperately to things that cause us constant frustration due to the fear it's the best we can get, to fear and despair.

The underlying fear related to this belief is, "What is going to happen to me?" You may recognize it in the following statements:

"What if I never achieve something better than what I've lost?"
"What if I never get what I want?"
"What if I get what I want and it doesn't fulfill my wishes?"
"What if the current situation lasts forever?"
"What if I am not in the right place at the right time?"
"What if I missed the chance?"

2. The belief that if people know who I really am, they will reject me.

The lack of unconditional love and the feelings of worthlessness we have developed over the course of our lives, have left many of us with the belief that we can't be loved just as we are, and thus, if someone does love us, something must be wrong with him or her.

The main fear behind this belief is that our image will crack and that everyone will be able to see who we really are.

The following fears lie beneath it:

- Fear of rejection
- Fear of failure
- Fear of what people might think or say about us
- Fear of the brutal judgment we inflict on ourselves
- Fear of facing our "failures" (avoiding a family gathering, for instance, in order not to encounter our married siblings)
- Fear of success (the real fear is not of success but of its outcomes; that we won't be able to live up to people's expectations or that success will soon be followed by failure).

The fear of facing what we perceive as evidence of our feelings of worthlessness is the fear of life itself. Those who are pursued by it use any excuse to avoid life, to avoid proof of their failure.

Moving Beyond Fear

As long as our actions are driven by the attempt to avoid possible unwanted outcomes, we strengthen our fears, as our message to ourselves is that there's something to fear. The reality of our lives is indeed full of challenges and uncertainty, yet anxiety over future events that we don't really know if, when, and how they will happen is a mindset that causes paralysis and confusion at the present moment, and consumes valuable energy we could have used to solve the problems we are facing. For example, naturally I fear the day that my mother dies, but as long as I'm dwelling on painful future scenarios, I'm missing the precious time we still have together. Even without the frightening scenarios, I know it will hurt, but as I'm creating no drama around it, I also know I will be able to cope in time. When facing financial difficulties, anxiety about the future won't help, as the energy it consumes at the present moment makes it difficult to focus on creative ways to supplement our income.

Overcoming fears such as stage fright, social phobias, or being true to ourselves lest we experience rejection, require taking action despite the fear. Many are waiting for the fear to dissolve (they have been waiting for years already) while trying to convince themselves there is nothing to fear. But without taking action and being willing to fail, their efforts remain futile. When the noise in our heads subsides and we can feel who we really are, the reluctance to try new things disappears, as our self-image can no longer be shattered by failure.

Nevertheless, the ability to break free from the lion's share of fear, as well as from different sorts of anxiety, lies in the understanding that fear is not a direct outcome of the circumstances but vice versa; initially fear exists as an energy, and only then it uses the circumstances as a fuel. Maybe it will be easier for you to understand this idea if you think of the fears of others, which often seem unreasonable and redundant. When we try to prove to someone that there is nothing to be afraid of, we find it hard to understand why he is not able to understand our logical explanations, because we fail to understand that his fears are just an expression of the energy of fear within him (or her).

That's why no rational explanation will lessen our fears for long, and definitely won't defeat them. The only thing that can overcome fear is presence. Not changing the circumstances, not the next thing that's supposed to make us happy, only presence. And when we truly understand it, our reluctance to practice presence dissolves.

Only presence can free us from our greatest fear—the fear of death, of annihilation. Regardless of your beliefs, only when you are fully present in the moment can you intuitively feel "the timelessness from which all time emerges," as Seth describes the eternity of life in Jane Roberts's book, *The Nature of the Psyche*.[4]

Sometimes, just when fear starts losing its grip, suddenly you find yourself sinking into a swirl of fearful thoughts, unable to break free, as if fear is trying to hold onto the horns of the altar. The phenomena called "intrusive thoughts"—which involves obsessive thinking about an unwanted objective (sometimes meaningless)—is also an expression of fear. I used to suffer from it from time to time, until one day, when such a thought refused to let go for longer than usual, I understood that as I fear it and attempt to suppress it, it only intensifies. Once I stopped fighting it, and when it came up I would only mention to myself, "Here comes the fear again," it was soon gone.

When fear fades away, even if it still raises its head from time to time, love arises.

Love

The power of love, which includes the rest of the powers within it, was given to humans by God as a symbol of his love for them. God wanted humans to feel as joyous as he felt when he created them and to always remember who they truly are. "This power," he said, smiling, "will bring abundance, happiness, and blessing into your lives and provide you with the ability to fulfill all your dreams."
~ From "The Five Wondrous Powers"

What is Love?

When people talk about love, they mainly refer to being in love. But being in love is not love, though we may learn to love the person whom we have fallen for.

It's almost impossible to put love into words. Maybe I can tell about the feelings it creates: a connection to life, to myself, and to others, empathy, acceptance, joy, serenity, clarity, and focus. Crying may arise out of compassion, intuition's voice is sharper, coincidences occur easily, and things turn out for the best without a guiding hand. And maybe I can tell about the moments it arises: looking with awe at the child I love; acknowledging the silent presence of my mother in her sleep; feeling the joy of returning to my favorite place, of my skis pressing against the snow; becoming immersed in a fascinating book; feeling the knowing inside me; loving a group of people with whom I share a journey because I see who they truly are and they see me; realizing I will always love the place where I grew up, though there was a time I hated it, and that I love my path in life despite the pain I've experienced; being free of myself for a moment; being there fully for another person and wanting everything for him or her; acting foolishly, laughing, and enjoying myself.

The Difference Between Love and Being in Love

Being in love connects two people in a wonderful rush of aliveness and happiness. It's one of the most exciting sensations humans can have, but the myth around it often creates frustration and suffering. The myth of the perfect love is presented in reality shows (in which the relationship usually ends in bitter disappointment shortly after the end of the show), movies, songs, and novels. The drama is intensified by unrealistic statements, such as "She is perfect" and "Forever," and by the promise of eternal love (which actually refers to the idea of being eternally in love).

The myth of the perfect love, which is called by mistake "true love," nourishes the pain that comes from the lack of unconditional love by promising, "Here comes the one who will always understand you, always love you, will accept each part of you and calm your anxious soul." That's why romantic love turns so quickly into an addiction to the sense of admiration we feel from our lover, to the interest he or she shows in us, and to the passion in his or her eyes. And that's why it's bound with fear; the fear that sooner or later the intoxicating drug of admiration will fade, that the hope of relieving our pain won't fulfill itself, and that another rejection, if it happens, will be conclusive evidence of what we really think—that we are not good enough, that we are worthless. And when fear sneaks into our hearts, the amazing feeling turns into a painful dependency that holds nothing but anger and disappointment.

Real love, unlike being in love, is not limited by capacity or time. If you loved someone, the love for him or her will always live in your heart, and you will always be able to visit it in your thoughts and dreams. It's free of needs, and it does not depend on the choices and actions of those you love.

Love is not a knowing but a feeling. Sometimes we know we love someone only because the thought about his or her possible death creates pain, though day by day we hardly ever feel our love for that person, as we are too busy with what he or she did to us or didn't do for us, or with resentment at his or her choices and behavior. Unsurprisingly, we find it easier to feel love for babies and pets, as we have no expectations from them. When we don't feel our love, it's as if it doesn't exist. Thus, after we behaved in an offensive way to a child or an adult, there is no point in saying, "You shouldn't feel offended; you know I love you," or, "It was all out of love," as love is not what this person experienced from us.

Loving behavior is not only what's considered as positivity, but it's always bound with respect for ourselves and for others and keeps the other person's best interest at heart.

Love is reciprocal. If you want to know how much someone loves you, all you need to do is to frankly ask yourself, "How much do I love him or her?" (contrary to "How much am I dependent on or obsessed with him or her?"). I truly understood this idea when I found out that the fur of the arctic bear is not white but transparent, and that its color is a reflection of the snow—the same way those around us reflect our feelings for them.

When love is the primary feeling present in the relationship, people will willingly listen to anything you say. When judgment, blame, and resentment rule, they will reflect back to you in the form of resistance and war.

Love, Abundance, and Fame

Why do so many people pursue wealth and fame? Because they confuse admiration with love. When the lights are turned toward them and the world looks up to them, they finally feel worthy and loved. But when their fame subsides, the terror of the feelings of worthlessness that are still inside them arises.

The essence of love is abundance; the essence of fear is misery. The way to bring true abundance into your life is to give up negativity, and through presence feel the love that is already within and around you.

Compassion

The most important part of the shift from fear to love is the awakening of compassion. Compassion is forgiveness toward other people's unconsciousness, as well as toward our own weaknesses. It arises when we realize that not everyone can understand and implement what seems logical, even if theoretically it could do them good and ease their suffering. It is based on the understanding that the awakening of mankind is a process, of all of us as a species and of each one of us as an individual. There are some who awaken and some who contribute to others' awakening through the intolerable pain caused by their unconscious actions. If they have chosen these lives in advance (and I believe they did), I salute them for their courage.

One Energy—How Everything Is Connected

"I rarely think about it," "It's only coming up now because we are talking about it," "What does my love life has to do with my relationships with my parents?"

The above sentences and the like, which I often hear from my clients, are based on the incorrect assumption that what we suppress does not exist, and that inside us there is a kind of inner compartmentalization—family, romance, health, work—without each being influenced by the emotional energy created by the other.

The energy inside us is one, as if it was water flowing and filling each corner. That's why it doesn't matter what its source is or how much it occupies your mind; all that matters is whether it's still alive. The answer to that may be found in the little moments: when a word of your parents makes you jump with anger and awakens old pain; when a question about your past makes you feel like a child again and feelings you have long forgotten come to life; when you find yourself offended and defending yourself, as deep down you believe in what has been said; when you are faced with something you believe your happiness depends upon; in the quiet moments and in your dreams.

To make the shift from fear to love and change our life circumstances, we should acknowledge every single piece of fear and pain that still lives within us and learn to look at it without judgment in order to see through the illusion it creates. The simplest way to detect this energy, which I've called "negativity," is by getting to know its two central axes—pain and fear.

The axis of pain is running between submissiveness and aggressiveness—submissive behavior stems from a desperate need for approval, which can easily trigger a sense of rejection, enormous pain, and feelings of guilt. The source of the guilt is in the way we interpreted our parents' emotions when we were children—we blamed ourselves for behaving in a way that made them sad, or we felt that by being "not enough..." (pretty, smart, etc.), we failed to make them happy. The reason that so many children feel guilty is that most parents lay the burden of their feelings on their children in an aggressive, disrespectful, and dismissive way, by using statements such as, "Why do I deserve this?" "I'm sick of you," or, "This is the thanks I get?" Parents can also make children feel guilty without words, through expectations that can never be satisfied.

Guilt encourages submissive behavior—the attempt to be "good" and to please in order to gain approval, and the fear of being "bad" lest we experience the pain of rejection again. But submissive behavior inevitably results in anger toward those who pushed us to act this way and failed to provide us with the approval we feel we so desperately need.

The pain and the anger accumulate and turn into a violent rage that seeks relief through self-destruction, illness, aggressive thoughts, or acts of physical and verbal abuse toward other human beings or life forms.

The axis of fear is running between blame and self-pity—when we blame, resent, or bear grudges against others, our righteous anger disguises the feeling of worthlessness, the scary thoughts, and the painful emotions that we dread. But at the same time, it strengthens our sense of victimhood and fills us with a violent energy that remains within us all the time, not only when we talk or think about the subject of these feelings. Thus, as long as we hold onto blame, our pain will intensify and our victim mentality will get stronger.

Often the most sensitive people become the most negative, self-destructive and aggressive. They were born with the thinnest membrane, with the ability to sense all that's around them—an amazing ability for empathy, compassion, and love. But when a small child encounters so much negativity, as currently this is the ruling energy of our culture, and his or her membrane is so thin, he or she cannot really deal with it. That's why the most sensitive children often turn into the most rigid adults; overly-sensitive, taking everything personally, full of negativity, and so deeply absorbed in their own pain that they are blind to the feelings and needs of anyone else. I know; I was like that.

The path to the amazing power of love is not through the attempt to be "more" (worthy, good, or full of love), simply because there's nothing to add. This power is already within you, within each one of you. It's there now. But as long as you are filling yourselves with negativity you cannot access it. Negativity is like muddy dirt that covers the magnificent diamond of who you truly are. That's why I'm urging you to look at the negativity you are creating, not because I want to hurt you or to make you feel bad about yourselves, but because I know that when you acknowledge it and give it up—you will have everything you want.

Emotions as an Inner Guide

Emotions are the most incredible gift humanity received, and the tool through which we create our reality. Our emotional frequency draws into our lives people and events that reflect what's inside us, determine the way people react to us, the way we perceive the world and respond to circumstances, and of course, the way we feel moment by moment.

Our emotions provide constant feedback about our

surroundings and serve as an inner compass. When we acknowledge them and listen to their guidance, the need to rely on external guidance disappears.

Our bodies, through sensations and appearance, teach us about the emotions that fill us: suffering emotional distress or lack of energy, looking worn-out, being overweight, physical pain, illness, and signs of premature aging attest to painful emotions of fear and negativity. Feelings of comfort, lightness, and health, a sound sleep, and a youthful and radiant appearance attest to inner peace and love.

Through attention to our bodily sensations and thoughts, we can learn what is happening within us at any given moment and what we are "cooking" for ourselves.

The attempt to avoid feelings in order to avoid pain resembles a person's decision to have a surgical procedure to remove his scent receptors so that he won't have to smell the smells he detests. He might have felt immediate relief when not having to smell the smoke of cigarettes, garbage, or sweat. But at the same time, he (or she) would lose the ability to enjoy the scent of air after the rain, the fragrance of spring flowers, the smell of passion, of a loved one, of a place that holds sweet memories, or the smell and taste of delicious foods. And this is exactly what you are doing—when you are trying to avoid pain, you are blocking the fullness of life—as emotions are the essence of life and acknowledging them, without drama, will prove you that even when they are painful, they can never take over you.

Chapter 7

Conscious Creation

People want change. They want to feel good, to be happy, and to enjoy life. But they are convinced that it won't be possible "until…" they find love and aren't so miserable and lonely anymore, their mom/dad/life partner/boss changes his or her ways and stops ruining their peace of mind, their children learn to respect and appreciate them and make the choices they think are right, they have enough money, annoying stuff like traffic jams or rude service providers stop wasting their time, or they finally think, feel, and behave the way they expect of themselves.

In fact, it would be more accurate to say that they want change but would rather wait until someone or something else does it for them—another person, circumstances that will suddenly work out, or a magic pill that will make everything simple all at once.

Eventually the pain forces us to acknowledge that we are creating our suffering with our own hands, not the circumstances. We attract certain people and events into our lives, we are responsible for the way people react to us, for things that recur in our lives, and for the challenges our children experience. Responsible, not guilty. In the same way that we are responsible for the good things in our lives.

When we realize that despite our best efforts nothing has really changed, the pain becomes intolerable and forces us to look for the relationship between cause and effect without self-judgment or blame, and then we suddenly realize that we have a choice after all, and that the easiest way to achieve what we want is the one we were so desperately trying to avoid—changing ourselves.

In the following chapter—that on the one hand holds enormous potential for change, but on the other hand may create enormous resistance—the truth will reveal itself, and you will no longer be able to ignore your creation and hold others accountable for your life circumstances.

Full Responsibility—Getting Control Back into Your Hands

We all create our own reality, but the greatest creators, those who live in peace and satisfaction and whose creation contributes to the greater good, are those who are aware of what they create and take full responsibility for their creation.

The meaning of full responsibility is to stop looking for evidence that we are not as bad as others, and instead to look for what we still need to change in ourselves.

It's to consider the predicted outcomes of our actions: of the way we treat others, even if only behind their backs; of the tone of voice we use, not only the words; and of the way we dress and show up.

It's to stop looking for reasons beyond our control for our situation and that of our children. No one is born with suicidal tendencies; pain drives people to become suicidal when they cannot stand it anymore. Teens don't get addicted to prescription drugs because it's a social trend, but because they are trying to run away from pain. And a child won't suffer anxiety or depression only due to personal disposition, unless he or she has been affected by his or her parents' mental and emotional health, their attitudes toward each other and toward him or her.

The meaning of full responsibility is to stop expecting that someone else will take responsibility for our lives. It's to understand that as adults we are solely responsible for our life circumstances, and to remember that even though we don't have full control over the ingredients life gives us, we can become "expert chefs"—those who create a gourmet meal with any raw materials they get.

Are You a Creator or a Victim?

Conscious creation requires a shift from the victim's to the creator's stance. Victimhood is deeply entrenched within the cultural pattern of guilt and blame. Guilt determines, "I feel guilty and I can't stand it." Blame determines, "If someone else is found guilty, it means I'm innocent."

By putting the blame on others we relieve feelings of guilt, but at the same time doing so enhances our sense of victimhood and intensifies the negative energy within us. And when instead of acknowledging the obstacle certain circumstances—such as skin color, gender, a challenging childhood, the nature of the people around us, or financial distress—may cause, we blame our circumstances, we present ourselves as helpless victims. Victimhood can also hide beneath seemingly innocent statements, such as, "But what can I do?" "Everyone around me...," or, "He forced me to do that." Such statements, even though presenting us as marionettes, free us from responsibility for our choices, and thus from the fear that we might have another thing to blame ourselves for.

Since guilt-tripping, shaming, and the tendency to lay the blame on others are in use all around us—at the heart of parent-child relationships, in politics, religion, in the army, and in the legacy of more than one nation—there is a confusion between personal responsibility and self-blame, because of which we are all afraid to be proven guilty in the sentence we hold for ourselves. This fear often manifests in the resentful reaction that so swiftly pops up when we advise someone to acknowledge his or her responsibility: "So I'm the one responsible for this?"

Whereas guilt is a natural emotion that serves as an inner direction mechanism that helps us learn from the consequences of our actions, self-blame is no more than a fictitious repair mechanism that says, "What kind of person am I if I don't feel guilty for what I've done?" as if a guilty conscience makes amends for what happened and serves as evidence of the offender's morality. But as long as the mother who hurt her children mourns her deeds, she is not available to provide them with the support they need now. The harsh self-judgment weakens her and affects her ability to cope with the situation, and her misery might encourage her children to try to comfort her.

In order to break free from the cycle of guilt and blame, you should understand that the world always reflects what's inside you; initially you blame yourself and agree that you are guilty, and only then your guilt is reflected as blame directed at you. When you acknowledge your responsibility and stop adding fuel to the fire with over-apologizing, self-justification, and counter-accusations, your reactions no longer feed the grievances of others.

There is no point in demanding unconscious people to acknowledge their responsibility. They wouldn't be able to distinguish between self-blame and responsibility even if you explained the difference. Freeing yourself from the victim stance and taking control of your life will only be possible when you are willing to see how heavy the burden of guilt they are already carrying is, and stop pushing them to admit it.

Did You Make Yourself Clear?

A common justification for complaining about others and blaming them stems from statements such as, "She was supposed to understand," "Why can't he think about it for himself?" "Instead of him I would...," or, "Any normal person would have...." Such statements represent the compulsive need to complain, blame, and make others wrong.

The expectation that other people will behave in a way that seems right to us and think in an identical way to ours is unrealistic. Besides, those who make such demands should first examine themselves to see if they act the same way they expect of others.

As long as we're waiting for another person to understand what he or she "should" do and how he or she is "supposed" to react, we remain in the victim stance. And when we are trying to clarify our expectations through manipulations such as silent treatments or demonstrations of sadness and anger, we're only intensifying our anger and creating frustration on the other side (even if the other person gives in and tries to please us so that we quit the manipulation).

"But why do I have to explain everything? Isn't it obvious?" you may ask. No, nothing is obvious, and you don't have to say anything, but if you want to live in choice and consciously create your reality, you'd better do so.

The Space in Which Relationships Are Formed

A client tells me about how tension developed between her and a friend of hers. On the surface it seems as if the distance built between them is a natural outcome of the circumstances, but underneath, accusations and self-justification are smoldering. "If only I change my attitude, nothing will happen," my client justifies her reluctance to give up the seemingly subtle battle she is conducting against her friend—the things she does just to spite her, and the fact she allows herself to discuss her friend's private affairs with whoever is willing to listen, while hiding under a facade of goodwill. Beneath her actions lies the fear of losing her beloved friend, but her unwillingness to take responsibility for the judgmental energy she is bringing into the space of the relationship only distances her further.

Another client is describing how her husband complains over and over again that she treats him as if he doesn't matter. "I don't care that he says so, because I know it's not true," she states angrily. She feels he is the one who is not showing empathy toward her, and thus she is not willing to acknowledge his feelings. She holds onto the idea that he should change first, while the vehicle for change is in her hands—acknowledging the influence of her actions on his feelings and reactions.

The assumption that both sides have to change to create

a change in a relationship is wrong. Each relationship forms an energetic space between the two involved, over which each has full control. Thus, even if the unconsciousness of the other person is deep and he or she cannot change him- or herself, when we no longer direct judgment, condemnation, and blame toward that person, his or her attitude toward us turns upside down.

The ability to influence the space of the relationship lies in the understanding that no side is completely innocent, no matter how it looks on the surface, no matter who was the first one to hurt the other, no matter if one seems sane and the other insane, if one is perceived as good and the other as bad, or if everyone agrees that one is right and the other is wrong—it's always both sides who are responsible for the space of the relationship. Therefore, you are the one who should take the first step—the one who is capable, the one who is fed up with anger and pain, the one who is actively choosing to change his or her life.

As long as we are not willing to accept other people's limitations, we create for ourselves a reality of constant frustration. "But she's a grown-up. I can't accept that she is not able to change," insists the daughter, justifying her judgmental attitude toward her mother. But there are things that for the daughter are simple and even obvious, that are beyond the mother's comprehension. "Only when you accept the situation will you be able to enjoy what she can offer and break free of the anger that sends you to the fridge over and over again," I tell her.

When it comes to destructive relationships we witness, there's a tendency to perceive one side as the abuser and the other as the victim. Yet many times such relationships last for years in a kind of a ritual, and despite their continuous complaints, the distorted relationship satisfies the needs of both sides, each of whom is, in fact, afraid to live without the other.

The Influence of Your Inner Energy on the Reality of Your Life

We all have the ability to feel the energy around us. Some places, for instance, make us feel suffocated and others open our hearts wide, some people make us feel good and others bad, and we can often tell what others are feeling even if they put on an act.

Our emotional energy radiates from within us, and even when people can't put what they feel into words, they find themselves reacting to it. The real communication is never verbal—we are not reacting to the words but to the energy behind them. Even so, time after time I hear people bitterly claim, "I really don't understand why he treats me like this. I really don't deserve it." "Listen to yourself and see how much disrespect, judgment, and blame you are expressing toward him," I say. "But I didn't show anything!" he or she defends. "Your words are meaningless. Your true feelings are felt by those you're interacting with, even if unconsciously, and impact the way they react to you," I explain what seems obvious to me now, though I know that it's not so at all.

Often clients ask, "So what was I supposed to do?" or, "What was I supposed to say?" "It really doesn't matter," I answer. "What matters is the energy behind your words and actions, not the words themselves." This energy has so much power that even a written word (an online comment, text message, or email) can easily transmit it.

Sometimes we try to pretend that everything is okay while suppressing frustration and fear. In one of the reality shows on Israeli television, a psychologist asked one of the participants, "Why aren't you sharing your feelings with your partner?" "I don't want to pin it on him; I don't want to be heavy," she answered. But even when she was trying to keep her feelings to herself, her gloominess, despair, and self-doubt were clearly felt, even through the screen, and affected her partner's reactions.

Whereas a constant smile and friendly behavior regardless of the circumstances will do the job and help their owners to be perceived as charming, even those employing this strategy won't be able to prevent their real emotional energy from influencing their intimate relationships.

People who say, "I'm too good," often conceal a deep sense of victimhood and resent those who "exploited" their kindness. They dismiss their wishes and needs for the benefit of others while justifying their choices with the claim, "I can't hurt another person." But this is only a nice story they tell themselves. Their true motive is to present an image of someone better than others, an image that justifies the grievances that go along with their "good deeds." Despite their giving, they are often criticized and exploited by others, because of the negative energy that accompanies their actions.

When people are hostile toward us or reject us for no apparent reason, it's due to one of two reasons: our negative attitude toward them, that affects their reactions even if we only express our feelings behind their backs or within ourselves, or energy of fear and violent rage that lives within us and "draws fire" even before we've said a word.

The Impact of Your Unrealistic Expectations on Your Relationships

Many relationships suffer from the burden of unrealistic expectations—the expectation that those around us will pay us their full attention, put us at the top of their priorities, and accept any behavior of ours without judgment—the same expectations our parents didn't fulfill. But when we lay the burden of our pain upon others, hoping for salvation, they might find it hard to bear and react aggressively in an attempt to fend off the demanding energy that never finds satisfaction. That is why many relationships, and especially romantic relationships which are considered as the key to happiness, fill quickly with mutual grudges, frustration, and pain.

When we let go of unrealistic expectations, we can suddenly see that it wasn't lack of love that made the other person step back but the energy he or she sensed from us. I had the opportunity to understand this when the expectations I'd laid on the shoulders of a good friend made her, following a meaningless incident, cut off contact with me for three years. When we renewed our relationship the burden has been removed and the impact was huge. Since then we no longer use every little thing as evidence of lack of care and love.

Only when we no longer expect others to fulfill our emotional needs and ease our pain, can we look at them clearly, see who they really are, what they are capable or incapable of, and if we choose to engage with them—we choose them for who they are, not for who we would have wanted them to be.

Tempting Moments of Satisfaction

There are various expressions of negativity, seemingly minor, that are widely accepted and even considered justified in our culture. If you try to explain to an unconscious person the negativity such expressions create, he or she will dismiss it offhand and might even accuse you of being judgmental toward him or her.

Complaining is one of the common expressions of negativity. During a "heart-to-heart talk" we complain about our parents, spouses, children, bosses, colleagues, friends, and more and more.

Some complain incessantly about the current person who is in the center of their dissatisfaction; others complain obsessively about everything—about other people's behavior, about their health, or about the television programs they keep watching. They are never satisfied. Some, instead of asking for what they want, just complain, expecting others to fix things for them, and some express their complaints even on their Facebook timeline: "Too much is missing..." or just "Ughhhh!"

And what's wrong with a totally justified complaint and blowing off some steam? The consequences involved. The negative energy these actions create, the need for self-enhancement at the expense of another they conceal, and the intensification of the victim identity in those who use these forms of expression. Complaining has nothing to do with acknowledging our feelings; it doesn't vent or clean anything; it only fuels our anger, misery, and pain.

The following quote from Israeli journalist Ayelet Shani,[5] addressed to her partner, illustrates brilliantly the common justification for negativity. "The worst nightmare of any grouchy person is to share his or her life with someone who is happy with his or her lot and believes that being angry is punishing yourself for other people's stupidity. 'I don't want you to calm me down; I don't want you to explain to me why I'm wrong. I just want to sulk and complain, and for you to nod in agreement and from time to time add some fuel to the fire. How many pleasures do I have in this life that you want to take this one away from me too?'"

But despite the amusing way in which things are presented, each expression of negativity adds to the accumulation of negativity within us, one drop after another, and this energy, in turn, influences our physical and emotional health, the way others react to us, and the nature of the people and events we attract into our lives.

The tempting little "treats," whose influence we overlook, are the main thing that stands in our way to greater, lasting satisfaction, which is always just within our reach.

The Far-Reaching Influence of the Energy Within Us

When we agree to do something and can't bring acceptance into the situation, our inner energy dramatically affects the events we experience. The following incident demonstrates it well. A year ago, while participating in a weekend workshop, one of the participants who lived next to me asked me to give her a ride back home. From the first moment I saw her I felt instinctively repelled, and after a busy day I was reluctant to take her with me, but still I said yes. We got back and I dropped her off at the corner of the street, hurrying to find a place to park my car. All of a sudden, a parking spot became available right behind me, and my hitchhiker was standing next to it. For a moment I hoped she would save it for me, but she turned on her way and someone else took the place.

I spent the following forty minutes looking for a parking place, but all my efforts were in vain. Eventually I parked at the corner of the street—where it's officially illegal but unofficially permitted during nighttime—with the intention to move my car within ten minutes to a nearby parking lot that was about to open. I went home for a couple of minutes and when I came back I found out that I'd gotten a parking ticket. Later I sent the municipality a request to cancel the ticket, but for the first time, after all my prior requests had been answered, I was declined. When reading the unfair rationale for the decline, I considered sending an appeal, but then I understood that the negative energy that accompanied my reluctance to give my classmate a ride resulted in this unfortunate sequence of events and that there was no point in dragging it out any further.

The Inner Zipper—The Power Source of the People We Look up To

The inner zipper is a metaphor for an inner state of choice, of willingness to handle our emotions even when they are turbulent, instead of demanding of others to take care of us and fix things for us. A person who uses his inner zipper (we all have one but most of us never zip it up) is someone who has found his inner source of power. When such a person experiences emotional turmoil, instead of looking for others to lift his spirits, he continues his daily routine calmly while looking inside for the inner grip that was temporarily lost. This person may as well get some support, yet he knows that the answer is always within him- (or herself).

During the leadership program I participated in a couple of years ago, I experienced a significant personal transformation, and things that seemed impossible up until then became suddenly effortless. One day during the morning ritual I remained gloomy and tears filled my eyes. At the group's discussion held after the ritual, one of my classmates gave me some feedback. "When you were crying during the morning ritual I was thinking to myself, 'Uh, Sharon again!'" she said. "We all experience difficulties here," she added, "but in your need for attention you are oblivious to the impact of your behavior and to other people's feelings." Despite my friend's concern not to hurt me, her words provided me with tremendous relief and became a turning point in my life. Until that moment I used to pity myself and considered myself the most miserable one who deserved special attention, but then I realized I didn't need or want it anymore. The feedback made it clear that if sympathy is what I'm looking for, my behavior only creates antagonism in others.

On my last vacation, I met a twenty-nine-year-old woman who had already married a great guy, given birth to a sweet baby, and graduated from medical school. Her relationship with her husband was something to which many aspire. She was pleasant but made no effort to please. She was genuinely interested in others and had the sense not to take every little thing personally. Some may think (as I used to think in the past) that because she has so much it's easy for her to be so pleasant, but it's the opposite—because she is so pleasant she has so much.

Feeling Your Own Negativity from Within

As clarity grows and inner peace intensifies, everything we experience becomes sharper. And so, if before we have downplayed the significance of seemingly minor expressions of negativity—such as complaining, mocking others, writing a vicious online comment or an aggressive email—by calling them "natural human expressions," now we no longer need explanations for why they are harmful. Because now that we can instantly feel the pain that the negativity we express creates within us, we simply don't want to do it to ourselves anymore.

What Do You Really Want?

The power of will was given to humans so they would be able to create anything they wanted. "Wish for something, get excited about it, visualize it as if it was real, and it will be yours," God said.
   ~ From "The Five Wondrous Powers"

Singles want loving relationships, married couples want a house, financial stability, children, more children, or simply to feel attractive and loved again. Parents want their children to be happy, and we all just want to feel good. So why does it seem that almost every action we take leads in the opposite direction? The bachelorette wastes years thinking about the one who left, forces herself to date the "right guy," or gets into a relationship with the one who will never be hers. Couples want love but often treat each other with disrespect. Parents, who more than anything want their children's happiness, insist on forcing their way, oblivious to the pain they create.

If at the moment of truth of any action, word, or choice you make, you will ask yourself, "What do I really want right now?" and answer honestly, often the answer will be something like, "I want to be right," "I want to feel superior (a better person, smarter, or more successful)," "Forget my troubles for a while," "Regain my dignity," "Pay him back," or, "Prove her wrong."

Such answers are not inappropriate or wrong, except that they never stand in line with the purpose you claim you want to achieve, the one that will make you fulfilled. And always, after a short moment of pleasure, they leave you with a feeling of emptiness, increase self-judgment, frustration, and pain.

Above or Below?

While we often have more or less than others: higher IQ, a bigger house, more money, fewer children, or fewer years of formal education, using such parameters to determine whether we are superior or inferior to others, more or less valuable as human beings, is something we all do. When we imply the inferiority of another person, we momentarily enhance our sense of self and break free from the feeling of worthlessness that still haunts us.

If you look carefully, you will notice that a large part of your actions is driven by the need to present yourself as better than others or to indicate their inferiority. You will be able to find it in the tone of your voice, in your facial expressions, in the nature of the words you are using, and by paying attention to the true motives that drive your behavior at the moment of truth.

Here are some examples of the way this behavioral pattern manifests in our daily lives:

- Demeaning another person by talking to him in a mocking, critical, or offensive way, talking about his faults with a third party, or criticizing him (or her) in our heads. "He should be admitted to a psychiatric ward," or, "I pity her."
- Pointing out the wrongs done to us while overlooking or downplaying the impact of our own actions—"I always

show interest in her, but she's making no effort to show interest in me," complains one of my clients about her mother-in-law. "Is it possible that your judgmental attitude toward her, even if only expressed behind her back, makes her stay away from you and treat you offensively?" I ask.

- Disparaging other people's achievements—"Diapers is all they can talk about," "How is it that the ugly ones always get married?" or, "He only promotes yes-men."
- Taking on a prestigious or noble role—One of my clients perceived herself as a good daughter due to her significant contribution to the family effort of treating her sick father. Her giving, though, was tainted with a lot of negativity toward her mother and sister, who weren't willing to give up their lives, and toward her father, for his negative attitude and the emotional manipulations he pulled on her. Resentment, self-pity, and a sense of victimhood filled her and damaged her life. Another took upon herself the role of the family mediator. She did it with a bitter complaint about the helplessness of her family members and about the burden they lay on her shoulders. But despite the suffering created by the situation, both of them were reluctant to give up the prestigious role that made them feel better, worthier, and more capable than those around them.
- Using allegedly justified derogatory nicknames, such as "sad little person" or "bad person." There are no small or bad people; there are only madness and violence that stem from the unconsciousness, the fear, and the pain that are ruling our culture.
- Minding other people's business—Conducting a war of justice with my father about his interference in my sister's life, or dealing with the way my mother runs her

life as she can be much happier "if only..." (no matter that my constant suggestions only make her feel bad about herself).
- A need to discipline others or to give advice, deriving a sense of self-importance from supporting someone who is in distress, or holding on to the "savior" role—the one who will take the other under his or her wings and supposedly solve all this person's problems ("but what will he do without me?").
- Looking for another person's faults without self-examination while justifying it by saying, "at least I'm not...."
- The strongest boost to our sense of self is achieved by blaming others. When we blame someone, the grudge we bear is always in the background, even when we don't think about it, providing us with a sense of superiority and righteousness on the one hand, while tainting our lives with destructive energy of anger and victimhood on the other.

The paradox is that self-enhancement at the expense of another—a behavioral pattern I call "fictitious self-enhancement"—not only provides no more than momentary satisfaction but creates intense negative energy and deepens our feelings of worthlessness.

Let's see how:
- While providing a sense of superiority, fictitious self-enhancement involves a negative attitude toward others and thus creates negative energy that remains within us for a long time. If, for instance, we've built this energy at work by bad-mouthing the boss, it goes home with us, affects our family and children, and draws into our lives

people and events that echo this energy.
- It drives unpleasant and even offensive reactions from those who feel our judgmental attitude, even when we are not expressing it aloud.
- Some of its expressions are so blatant that afterward we feel ashamed of ourselves.
- Some feel guilty for the pain they caused others.
- And contrary to its original purpose—feeling better than others—each act of fictitious self-enhancement deepens our feelings of worthlessness. As by using this tactic, behind the scenes we are sending ourselves a decisive message. "I am small and unworthy, and therefore I have to continuously feed my sense of superiority." Since we are all born whole, it's only when we no longer try to prove to ourselves that we are good enough, that we can feel our wholeness.

Do You Want Love or War?

Many couples, parents and children, siblings and colleagues live in an ongoing situation that can be defined as a state of war—a state of mutual hostility with moments of truce. Conflicts in relationships often come from a yearning for approval, acceptance, and love, and the ones we are fighting are those who hurt us, disapprove of us, or threatened to deny us of something—the love, appreciation, or time of another person, or the promotion we've longed for. The son insists on punishing his father ("If I forgive him, it's as if I approve of all he's done over the years"), and the employee, instead of focusing on what she needs to do in order to get a promotion, launches an all-out war against her colleague who has been promoted ahead of her.

In a state of war there is no place for love. We can no longer see the humanity of our "enemy," and the motive that was initially a yearning for love trades places with the urge to hurt.

Any state of war is shared by both sides, even if on the surface one of them seems an innocent victim. A one-sided battle cannot go on for long, as we cannot fight someone who doesn't hold grudges against us and doesn't fight back. The strategy of the "innocent victim" may seem ostensibly justified, be sophisticated or obscured, often apparent only to his or her opponent.

The exception is the relationships between parents and their young children. Although a young child cannot be considered an equal partner in the relationship, sometimes a state of war is created between a child and one of her parents. The child fights the parent, avenges the lack of attention and rejection she experiences from the parent, the pain of her siblings being preferred, or disrespectful behavior toward her. The child's fight might be expressed in various ways. She may declare a preference for the other parent, demonstrate disappointment when she has to spend time with the parent she is fighting against, ignore the parent's requests, behave defiantly, and talk back. Her parent gets offended when he believes that the child doesn't love him, and thus stays away from her and prefers the company of her brother or sister who doesn't make him feel rejected. When the old pain awakens in the parent and says, "Here is another proof that you are worthy of nothing; even as a parent you've failed," the parent becomes blind to the child's needs and cannot see that the child fights to gain his love.

The need for war comes from a sense of inferiority and

pain, and those we fight are only the current players in our personal dramas. Until we have dealt with our emotional pain, even if one "enemy" leaves our lives, another swiftly fills the place.

Do You Want Forgiveness or Revenge?

Can you forgive a cheater? Someone who hurt you? In such situations we often force the other side to constantly please us in order to prove his or her love and redeem him- or herself. But no matter how hard he or she tries, it never satisfies our endless demands and the hole inside us never fills up.

The choice to stay in a relationship with someone who hurt you, hold that person's actions against him or her, and make his or her life miserable, though providing some comfort, comes at a high price—constant anger, recurring conflicts, hopelessness, despair, and a lot of pain.

When people say, "I forgive but not forget," they actually mean, "I don't forgive you, and I surely won't forget to show you that."

Choosing a life of revenge only for the momentary satisfaction it provides is a miserable choice. Stay and forgive; see what you can learn from what happened and look for the part you played in it. Otherwise, leave, despite the joint property, the kids, or anything else. Staying does not make you a noble person, it only causes suffering for yourself and for those around you.

What Do You Want at the Moment of Truth?

When someone says, "I want to, but..." and follows it with "I just don't do anything about it" or "I'm scared to do something about it," it's not the truth but a complaint about the situation. All those "want but…" statements justify the choices we consider as inappropriate and serve as an excuse not to give up the profit concealed in the current situation. There is nothing we keep or avoid doing without profiting from it.

If we acknowledged our ulterior motives, it would likely sound like this, "I want to break up with my married lover, but I'm not willing to give up the thrill the relationship provides," "My children are important to me, but right now it's more important to me to hurt my husband despite the price they are paying," or, "I want a good relationship with my wife, but I don't feel like giving up the sense of superiority I'm gaining from showing her how ridiculous her behavior is."

What we say we wish for is obviously something we truly want, but too often, at the moment of truth it's still a lie. How can we know that? Our words, choices, and actions will testify to our true desires.

In order to move toward our declared goals, we should first acknowledge the desires that rule at the moment of truth and, if needed, give them permission, no matter how crazy, bizarre, or wrong they seem—as this is where our hearts and energy go anyway. When we refuse to acknowledge our true motives, it gains us the right to resent our cruel fate and blame the world for preventing us from having what we wanted (though we got exactly what we aimed for).

The first step toward overcoming any unwanted situation is to fully acknowledge it. "Right now, all I want is to make my husband feel bad about himself," "Right now I want to prove I'm right," or, "Right now I long for a thrill no matter the cost."

Contrary to reason, it's only when we acknowledge our

true motives without self-condemnation that the door toward fast-tracked change suddenly opens.

The Small Life; The Big Life

The biggest obstacle to a life of happiness and choice is holding on to grudges, self-pity, and self-enhancement at the expense of another—three aspects that are actually one, the heart of negativity and the greatest key for change.

There is no one who wouldn't want the outcomes that can be gained by giving these up—serenity, true positivity, free energy that allows motivation and creativity to flow; a different, more positive attitude from those around us; and, of course, self-acceptance and love. But most of us are not willing to give them up without knowing for certain how we will profit from it. And that is how the short-term satisfaction these destructive behavior patterns provide turns into the biggest obstacle that stands in the way of those who are unable to reach what they long for. This is the barrier between what I've learned to call "the small life" (life full of fear and despair) and the "big life" (life full of love and happiness). Time and time again I see people fall into the trap and at the moment of truth refuse to give up the short-term satisfaction these self-defeating behaviors provide, fearing to be left with nothing.

Few are those who admit they are still not ready to let go of the unholy trinity, others just disappear, and those who are ready to awaken sit in front of me. "It's so hard," they say in tears, and I know it seems so, as once I was there, and though I don't feel this way anymore, I remember how hard it was. But the difficulty is not what it seems to be; not giving up is hard, but the unbearable burden of constant anger, the brutal fluctuations between feelings of superiority and even hatred toward others and feelings of worthlessness and inferiority, the paralyzing fear that stems from identification with the thought that my situation is the worst and that nothing will ever change, and the distorted perception of reality through the veil of thoughts that creates so much pain.

Just before giving up it seems impossible, but when we take the internal step it's so easy, and it changes everything. Everything. Sometimes it seems to me that no matter how many words I use, I will never be able to accurately express how meaningless my worldly achievements are when I have so much of what I always wanted and never believed I could have—love for myself, for others, ability to forgive, self-control, a sense of wholeness, serenity, and choice, 100% choice.

Conscious Choices and Sensible Decision-Making

A mother who says to her child, "I gave up my life for you," is speaking nonsense. In basic terms such a mother believes, no matter what she says, that she did not have that much to give up, and the "giving up" gave her a life that she wanted.

A child who says, "I gave up my life for my parents and devoted myself to their care," means, "I was afraid to live my own life, and afraid to let them live theirs. And so in 'giving up' my life I gained the life I wanted."

Love does not demand sacrifice. Those who fear to affirm their own being also fear to let others live for themselves. You do not help your children by keeping them chained to you, but you do not help your aged parents either by encouraging their sense of helplessness.

~ Jane Roberts, The Nature of Personal Reality. A Seth Book

When we don't take responsibility for our choices, it gives us the justification to blame someone else for the results we are getting or to complain about our misfortune. In fact, we are always making choices, even when we insist we are not—our choices are the actions we have taken or the ones we have avoided.

If we were willing to take responsibility for our choices, we'd be left with no justification for self-pity and blame. Some might say that free will is an illusion and keep complaining about their choices while justifying them: "I can't leave my job; I have responsibilities," meaning, "I'm afraid to leave my job and I'm not willing to give up the security it provides, but I'm not willing to stop complaining about it either," or, "I can't just walk away; there are children involved," meaning, "I'm too afraid to take the step and the story about the best interest of my children allows me not to admit it."

The Key to Wise Choices

Although in practice we are always making choices, the mental condition of not making a choice has a huge impact on our sense of happiness and satisfaction, and on our ability to recruit inner resources to support a desired change. The expression "one foot here and one foot there," means to literally be in one place while, in our minds, constantly planning on leaving. Many are keeping a job or staying in a relationship for years, and while "voting with their feet" on their choice to stay where they are, in their heads they keep complaining about the situation, and once again telling themselves, "I'm just about to leave." But despite their continued complaints, the current situation conceals advantages they are not willing to give up yet.

A wise choice is one that comes from a state of acceptance, and determines, "Despite the disadvantages of the current situation, this is the best choice I can make right now, and thus I'll give up complaining and choose to mentally be where I am." When we constantly complain we learn to believe our words, and find it hard to see that our inner resistance to the situation creates most of the suffering, not the situation itself.

To bring acceptance to a certain situation is to accept the current moment as it is without complaining, and then the next moment, and so on, until we are ready to choose otherwise. When we are no longer wasting energy with stories about "being stuck" and about the scary future that awaits, we can think more clearly and become more effective at achieving our goals.

It's Not Done Until It's Done

Though sometimes our choices seem unreasonable—to stay in a relationship despite the compromises it requires, in a job that doesn't lead to a clear career path, or in an apartment that does not fully satisfy our needs—everything in life has its own duration and every experience comes to teach us something. That's why any attempt to move on before our inner guidance agrees it's time involves a useless inner struggle. But due to the constant pressure to do the "right" thing, to "move forward" and not to "remain stuck," we tend not to listen to our inner guidance. And so, the husband once again tells his wife that he'll leave if she won't change her ways, but then returns shortly after with his tail between his legs, and the employee threatens to resign again, but her boss already knows it's a futile threat. If instead of going against their gut feeling they would ask themselves a simple question, "Is it over for me yet?" or, "Am I done here?" and answer frankly, they would save so much energy, frustration, and precious time.

Sensible Decision-Making

Most people make choices or avoid them out of fear. "I'm afraid to make the wrong choice," they say and remain stuck in their place, or they make a choice and can't stop wondering whether it was the wrong one. The fear associated with decision-making, however, is not due to its predicted outcomes. Instead, it lies in fear-based thinking patterns—beforehand we look into the future and automatically draw the worst-case scenario in our minds; afterward we look back and imagine how the decision we didn't make could have brought us much better results.

At a seminar I attended, the facilitator told a story that served as a turning point in decision-making for me. "Two people decided to try their luck in New York. One of them used his best efforts and became a successful business owner. The other, who thought that with this change his problems would finally be solved, became bitter when he found out that here, too, he had to make an effort to achieve success. He didn't manage to build financial stability and blamed himself for the decision he made."

The story emphasizes how meaningless the moment of choice is, and how important what we choose to do afterward is. It reminded me of an experience I had as a child. On a family trip I was sitting on the bus next to my parents, and my sister was sitting with our cousins. When I saw them enjoying time together, I got jealous and asked to switch places with her. My sister agreed. But when she was sitting with our parents, suddenly it seemed much better over there. While she accepted both choices willingly and thus made the best of them, I expected the circumstances to solve the dissatisfaction in me and thus felt disappointed with both choices.

Sensible decision-making is possible only when we listen to the direction provided by our emotions, yet most of us ignore it; we insist on acting out of pressure with the excuse, "Doing something is better than doing nothing," and force ourselves to stick to our decisions even when it's clear to us that they are not right for us (because giving up is a weakness, isn't it?). But it's only when we allow uncertainty that the clear answer comes in its time and the right action reveals itself.

The way to break free from the vicious circle created by the thinking mind is to start making decisions without looking back, except for learning. Many blame themselves for years for the choices they made. "It was a bad decision. I shouldn't have made it," they complain. "I made it for the wrong reasons," they add. They repeat it again and again, in their heads and aloud, filling themselves with sorrow and pain. The fact is that each decision you ever made was the best one you could have at the time. (If you are arguing with my claim, try to think if ever at the moment of truth you told yourself, "Okay, I'm going to make a stupid decision just for fun.") But even if you insist that I'm wrong, the past cannot be changed, and when we stop dwelling on "What if...?" the pain starts to dissolve and vital energy that allows us to deal more effectively with our current circumstances becomes available.

Inner Resonance

Inner resonance is the feeling that was present when you didn't feel the need to consult anyone, simply because you knew what was right for you. This feeling serves as a compass for the best choice for us.

You may identify its absence upon the inner argument that starts when you try to make the "right" decision despite your inner resistance. Then, in one fell swoop, you make yourself dumb, weak, or a coward—anything that supports the decision that seems right and justifies ignoring your inner voice.

Sometimes a certain decision immediately resonates with you; at other times you discover what's right for you only after you start moving in a certain direction and inner resistance appears, suggesting you should change your path.

Inner resonance does not require perfection. It can come with the decision to take the job that feels right despite the cut in pay, or to share a life with an imperfect partner while consciously accepting his or her flaws.

The Foundation of Self-Acceptance

There are lots of ways in which we are working against ourselves, overlooking our wishes, needs, opinions, and what really matters to us. We do it in order to feel good about ourselves, to maintain a positive image in the eyes of the world, to win people's love or not to lose it, or to achieve the goals we believe will make us happy. But as long as our actions are driven by fear and involve the denial of our true selves, they cannot help us in achieving our innermost desire—to truly love ourselves and be loved exactly as we are.

Embracing the Essence of Who You Are

The strict criteria about right and wrong and good and bad dictate who we should be to be socially accepted. Those strict criteria force us to wear masks and make constant efforts to adjust ourselves to the norms in order to feel worthy and gain approval. Few are those who can say wholeheartedly that they truly accept themselves, that is, that they live in peace with who they truly are.

As long as I can remember, I longed to be one of those cute and smiley people who captivate people's hearts. For years I tried to change myself and dreamed of the day I would be a different person, until the leadership program I took with CTI. One of the first assignments we had was to characterize our group members based on their initial impact on others. I was characterized as "Danger," the kind of person who might create discomfort in others, who sees the truth and dares to say it aloud in order to heal the wounds, who likes thrills and is willing to take risks, who in his or her own way creates a sense of security in others and grants them courage In short—me. During the program, I had the opportunity to experience the beneficial influence of my qualities and the power they conceal. I also had the chance to find out that over time people learn to know the variety of my qualities, not only the most prominent ones, when I got the "best smile" award from my classmates on graduation day—not one of the three people who were characterized with "Charm," the smiley type of person I always longed to be.

A client who went through a significant transformation,

the main part of which was to embrace the essence of who she is, told me, "At the beginning of our work together I wanted you to help me become the person I thought I should be. Though I don't enjoy working as a wage earner, I thought I should learn to love it as it seems the right thing to do. I also wanted to enjoy a job that involves leading a team, as it's considered prestigious." Despite those thoughts, she made her choices upon her heart's desire. Before we met, however, she believed that something was wrong with her, not because she didn't enjoy her life, but because she felt she was not complying with society's norms.

When we try to force ourselves to do something only because it seems right, even if we manage to do so we experience frustration and even suffering. Self-acceptance means working with ourselves instead of against ourselves, and accepting who we are instead of spending a lifetime trying to be somebody else. Only then, instead of being an obstacle, our natural qualities become the source of our true power.

Becoming an Independent Thinker

You are a multidimensional personality, and within you lies all the knowledge about yourself, your challenges and problems, that you will ever need to know. Others can help you in their own way, and at certain levels of development such help is necessary and good. But my mission is to remind you of the incredible power within your own being, and to encourage you to recognize and use it.

~ Jane Roberts, *The Nature of Personal Reality. A Seth Book*

"You are annoying," my client says, frowning. "You are telling me to stop pitying myself, but you are not telling me how to do it."

"Because there's nothing to add to what I've already said," I answer. "The key is simply to want it."

On the one hand, people want to feel worthy and confident, but on the other hand, they insist on being treated like helpless children. They constantly look for someone to tell them what to do, what decision to make, what to say, and how to behave in each and every situation. They refuse to acknowledge the contradiction it creates. "But I don't know what to do," they complain. "I'm afraid to be wrong," they add.

In fact, it's not that we don't know what to do; it's that we don't dare to give ourselves permission to do what feels right or to question the norms and the words of those we perceive as superior to us. Since our culture encourages conformism and obedience, rewards those who comply with the norms with respect and recognition, and condemns uniqueness, most of us turn into obedient adults who don't even dare to assume they know better than a specialist or a book. When we do not dare to think independently, we automatically place ourselves as inferiors to those whose opinions we accept as a fact, just like the child who believes that what his or her mother says must be true.

The importance of questioning everything and using my own judgment became clear to me through my interaction with the medical establishment. During the nineties, as a student, I started using computers, and soon my eyes turned itchy and red. In an attempt to solve the problem, I turned to several ophthalmologists who dismissed offhand the connection I'd made between working with computers and my irritated eyes, and diagnosed me with conjunctivitis. One after another they wrote me prescriptions for all kinds of eye drops, but to no avail. At a certain point I understood that this is not where my salvation would come from, and I solved the problem with a warm or cold compress I use every morning to calm my eyes. When I suffered from severe hair loss, the doctor dismissed it with the explanation, "It's because you are going outside with wet hair." He overlooked the fact that at that time I had been going out with wet hair for more than ten years, and that it never caused me hair loss before. Psychologists who advised me, without knowing me well enough, to solve my anger with psychiatric drugs, made it even clearer that I should question even what those who formally acquired the title "expert" say.

When I was assigned a senior position in finance, a field in which I had no prior experience or formal education, and yet fulfilled the role successfully, I learned that intelligence and common sense might be more important than formal education.

Independent thinking requires doubting everything before we fully understand it from within. "My therapist said," says a friend, supplying a theoretical explanation about her child's condition. "But what do you think? What do you see?" I ask. "He said…," "She said…," people mechanically quote the words of others instead of trying to see what they are thinking, what they are seeing, and what's right for them. The meaning of independent thinking is that even what I agree with, I want to make mine—to say it in my own words, to see it in my life and the lives of those around me, and if needed, to add to it or change it. That is, to know it from within.

Only when we no longer automatically accept the opinions of others and consider them as superior to us, we regain our freedom. There are areas where it's relatively easy for us, and areas where we find it hard to go against the stream. Dating is one of the areas in which there's a lot of pressure, especially on women, to give up their needs, preferences, and desires. The social pressure creates enormous fear and constant self-doubt in them and makes them believe that their demands are beyond reason.

When you dare to think independently, there will always be someone who says you are crazy, mocks you, gets furious with you, or tries everything in his or her power to "get you back on track," as there are many for whom a person who finds the ability to think independently becomes a serious threat. But in order to become aware of your strength and find the path to the wisdom that is already within you, you have to dare to think for yourself.

Listening to Your Inner Guidance

There is a voice within each of us that always guides us. It might say, "Do this," or, "Don't do that," or give us a gut feeling. It provides guidance about matters of great importance as well as about daily matters. Most of the time we ignore it, but often we find ourselves thinking in retrospect, "Why didn't I listen to myself??"

Before we learn to be present, the constant noise in our heads makes it difficult to discern our inner voice from the rest of the voices that never rest (the voice of fear, the voice of the norms, or the voices of our parents), and when we constantly seek advice, our inner noise strengthens, as well as the fear of trusting ourselves. One of my clients expressed it well: "Taking advice from too many people left me confused and made it impossible for me to understand what I really feel."

As we become more present and still, our inner voice sharpens. And when we start listening to it, we find the answers that are already within us and become our own authority. Then, we no longer need to put anyone above us.

The Hidden Power of Self-Permission

"I'm allowed to think what I'm thinking; I'm allowed to feel what I'm feeling; I'm allowed to want whatever I want."

The above sentence, which today seems obvious to me, aroused interest in a seminar I delivered. A young man in his twenties told me, "Out of the hour and a half you've spoken, this was what influenced me the most." Behind this seemingly innocent sentence lies the reason why so many of us believe that something is wrong with us, judge ourselves, and try throughout our entire lives to be someone else.

If you look into it, you will find that whenever the word "forbidden" is used, instead of helping, it works as a sign that says, "Turn your attention here!" A desire for a certain food that we strictly forbid, for instance, results in continuous thoughts about it and ends with overeating.

Any attempt to restrict or deny our thoughts and emotions creates an internal infection of forbidden thoughts and suppressed emotions that eventually leads to uncontrollable, offensive, or violent behavior, whether toward ourselves or toward others.

Self-Pride—Is It Really Bad?

One of the ways social norms encourage self-oppression is through the condemnation of self-pride, by calling it vanity.

When someone constantly talks about himself people say that he is in love with himself, but such a person doesn't love himself at all. As deep within he feels unworthy, he is trying to strengthen his sense of self by repeating his achievements and virtues in order to get validation of his worth from others. But since the soothing effect each validation provides doesn't last long, he (or she) needs to go on and on.

Self-pride—the willingness to acknowledge our strengths and achievements—is completely different, it is simply an act of self-love and joy. A young child naturally shows pride in his or her success, he or she looks around and proudly declares, "Look Mom, I made it!"

When a friend to whom I gave a ride mentioned, "You are so calm; for me driving is like a battlefield," I noticed how much I've changed. When a colleague spoke about his complicated relationship with his brother, I understood how precious and unobvious my relationship with my sister is. When I see around me the stress, pain, and negativity that were once my lot, I feel satisfaction and take pride in what I've accomplished. Usually I won't mention it to anyone, yet I won't apologize and will allow myself to enjoy it if my accomplishments are publicly recognized.

The World as a Giant Mirror That Reflects What's Inside Us

We usually think of the world as something fixed and solid over which we have little control, and of the events occurring in our lives as arbitrary. But in-depth examination reveals that it is more accurate to describe the world as a giant mirror that reflects what is happening inside us, as individuals and as a collective.

The reflection we see in front of us is the way the world allows us to learn from what we create, and if needed, to change it. Let's see how.

A Mirror of Our Beliefs

Beliefs are assumptions about reality that we perceive as truth. Most beliefs are rooted in reality and enjoy broad consent, so it's hard to doubt them.

We all have plenty of beliefs in various areas; we may desire financial abundance, yet carry a belief that winning the lottery is not an appropriate way to achieve it, or we may long for a romantic relationship, but deep down believe that all relationships end in frustration and pain. Our beliefs shape our reality and affect the way we perceive the world. A business owner who believes it's hard to attract new clients, experiences exactly that. Those who believe that the economic slowdown will affect their business, see their fears come true while others experience prosperity under the same circumstances. And when someone believes it will be difficult for him or her to find a relationship, he or she experiences frustration and lack. We strengthen our identification with our beliefs when we supply excuses for their reflection in our lives. "Most men can't handle a strong woman like me," "It's hard to succeed as a business owner," or, "There's nothing I can do; it's the economy."

Our beliefs are influenced by the belief systems of our society, that, for example, judge one person as better than another due to his or her origin, status, gender, skin color, age, weight, level of education, residence, or sexual preferences, and determine, according to such parameters, what's possible for this person. Other, more personal beliefs are the result of unintended "hypnosis" process done by those around us. For example, when my mother used to introduce my sister and me, she would say, "Sharon is the shy one." Sometimes she would tell us, "You are no athletes, just like me." Those statements and the like shaped my beliefs regarding my nature and abilities. And though over the years certain events have supported these beliefs and others have not, it took me a long time to fully realize that they were not true.

When a mystic declares that the next person that will come into your life is your last chance for love, that you missed the love of your life, or that you will never be rich, his or her words easily turn into a belief from which it might be challenging for you to break free.

In chapter 9 I will get into details on how to overcome limiting beliefs; for now, start identifying them and look through the illusion they create.

A Mirror of Our Self-Perception

Over the years I found myself in relationships with unavailable men. I thought it was simply bad luck, but the recurrence of similar events forced me to face the fact that it can't be a coincidence, even before I understood why it was happening. I knew those men had genuine feelings for me, yet they didn't choose me as their partner. Today I understand that initially I was the one who didn't choose herself. Even though I did appreciate myself in many ways, eventually I would always judge myself as not good or pretty enough, always less than someone else, always wanting to be somebody else. The men in my life simply reflected my self-perception.

In the same way, this time to my favor, the world always provided me with a confirmation of my wisdom. The first thing that people say when they get to know me is, "Sharon is smart." Even during high school, when I was struggling with learning because of the social difficulties I was facing, I was told again and again: "If only you had wanted to, you could have done much better." Here too, I was initially the one who didn't doubt her wisdom, despite the circumstances.

A Mirror of Our Attitude Toward Ourselves

The attitude we get from others always mirrors our attitude toward ourselves. Initially we overlook our needs and desires, and then we resent others for taking advantage of us. Initially we doubt our abilities, and then we feel offended when those around us doubt us. Initially we teach others that no matter how they behave we will always be there for them, and then we get furious when they take us for granted.

A certain attitude that recurs in our lives is simply the way that the world teaches us about our attitude toward ourselves.

A Mirror of Our Self-Judgment

The way other people judge us is often no more than the way we judge ourselves through the eyes of others. "She probably thinks I'm this or that…" we say to ourselves, and then we see exactly what we expect. When we are ashamed of something such as our age, our marital status, having been fired, or the number of children we have, we constantly see it in front of us—everyone asks, judges, or pities us. Once we cease apologizing for our "faults," either literally or only within ourselves, miraculously others stop judging us as well. It's not possible to feel sorry for someone who doesn't feel sorry for him- or herself, or at least there's no point in it—as we cannot derive a sense of superiority from it if he or she doesn't feel bad about his or her condition.

A large part of the judgmental dialogue is within ourselves. Often a client is quick to declare, "I know what you are going to say about it," and then supplies an answer she believes I would give, an answer that reflects her judgment toward herself.

If you are worried about the question, "What will people think of me?" the answer is simple—whatever you think of yourself.

A Mirror of Who We Are

When I say, "a mirror of who we are," it's not our innate nature that I'm talking about, but behavioral patterns that we are not willing to acknowledge or whose importance we belittle.

Often we harshly condemn others—their behavior, conflicts, and stupid choices—that are not that much different from ours; the friend who cannot admit her mistakes, who obsessively justifies herself and only thinks of herself (just like us), and the other, who is so deeply absorbed in her own pain (just like us) that she can't even give the needed attention to her children.

Single women who bitterly complain about the disrespectful behavior of the men they are dating, disregard the fact that often they allow themselves to act in the same way toward their friends, parents, or other men they are not interested in—they may ignore calls, cancel plans at the last minute, and provide unreliable excuses.

The way to earn respect is not to demand it, but to respect yourself and everyone else.

A Mirror of the Way We Treat Others

At the second retreat of the leadership program I took, I sat in front of the group, tears in my eyes, and accused them, "You don't love me!" But since I was determined to figure out what in me brought me the unwanted results I was experiencing, I forced myself to look through the illusion, and noticed that I was the one who was judging them, I was staying away from them, I was showing no interest in them, I was the one who was not expressing love toward them. And though it was due to my fear of rejection, still I was the one creating the results I was complaining about. It was my pain-colored glasses that screamed in my head that here's another proof for the fact that nobody likes me. Only when I remained still, looking and listening, I managed to see how badly these glasses distorted my perception.

A while ago, about an hour away from home, I suddenly noticed that my car was about to break down. I kept driving to the nearest gas station, knowing I would find someone to help me, and so it was. When I understood I needed to call a tow truck, I wasn't worried, as I was certain I would find a ride home, and sure enough, the third person I approached, a pleasant young man, agreed to give me a ride. Though it was an unwanted event, it ended with a great feeling. I found out that people are just waiting for you to trust them, see the best in them, and treat them with friendship and respect as equals, regardless of their gender, religion, occupation, or anything else. And when that happens, they will do anything for you.

A Mirror of the Soul of the Masses

The morning starts with several news stories about a violent weekend, during which different groups of teenagers have committed murders. On the television, the experts repeat the known arguments: "The media is the source of violence," "It's because of the drinking culture," or, "The problem is lack of education." And the solution they offer? To increase police enforcement.

But violence is not an outcome of impaired values or lack of enforcement, and it's not manifested only through the escalation of homicide rates, school bullying, or animal abuse. Many parents are witnessing violence in children and teenagers in their own homes when the child expresses extreme frustration and rage.

Is it alcohol's fault? No. Alcohol only loosens brakes and reveals what lies beneath the surface. Does television have a negative influence? It does. Fueling the drama between participants is what brings rating to reality shows. Some realities document the lives of celebrities, and though it's quite obvious that the participants feel emptiness and dissatisfaction with themselves and their lives, many feel unworthy in the face of their glamorous lives and see them as role models. Is there a connection between education and violence? Yes. The race to success drives self-judgment and deepens feelings of worthlessness in the weak, which in turn increase violent rage and the need for power.

Youth violence is nothing but a mirror of the soul of

the masses* and, mostly, of their parents' emotional state. Thus, a child who enjoys a stable home environment will be able to maintain his or her inner stability even in the eye of the storm.

Relationships as a Mirror

The most obvious way in which the world is putting a mirror in front of us is through our romantic relationships and through the emotional health of our children.

When talking about successful relationships, experts often emphasize the importance of making a wise choice, and, therefore, recommend creating a list of virtues of the desired partner in order to avoid mistakes. But even if on the surface our choice seems to meet all criteria listed up front, often we find ourselves once again in a relationship that involves disappointment and pain.

The reason for that is simple—no matter how hard we try to choose a strong and confident person who will be our rock and make us feel worthy, eventually we find ourselves with someone who seems to be our dream partner, yet his or her inner state accurately reflects ours; the level of pain he or she carries is similar to ours, his or her sense of worthlessness is as deep as ours, he or she is as fragile and vulnerable as we are, yearns for acceptance just like us, and the level of anger he or she suppresses resembles the level of anger we are struggling to control.

When two people are in a long-term relationship, it indicates that the intensity of their emotional burdens is

---

* The term "soul of the masses" refers to the cumulative emotional energy of a group, a country, and the entire planet, and their influence on the individual.

similar, otherwise the relationship wouldn't last. If one of them experiences an inner shift, he or she won't be able to remain in the relationship—he or she will find him- or herself ending it consciously or sabotaging it and unconsciously bringing it to an end.

In order to create the relationship you dream of, you should first become the person you want to attract into your life, as it's true that like attracts like.

The Path to Self-Love

What is done to you is what you are doing to others; thus, the path to self-love and to be treated with love is to stop blaming, judging, and bad-mouthing others. You don't have to say that everyone is flawless—it's obviously not the case—just stop using people's unconsciousness, faults, and failures to enhance your sense of self.

When acceptance and love reflect in front of you, you will know that this is what's inside of you. The idea is to first change ourselves and take responsibility on our impact on others, especially when our minds try so hard to convince us that we're only innocent victims.

Becoming Free of the Need for Control

Love always involves freedom. If a man says he loves you and yet denies you your freedom, then you often hate him.
  ~ Jane Roberts, Seth Speaks: The Eternal Validity of the Soul

Freedom is an integral part of our innate nature. When we deprive ourselves of it and try to adjust to the norms that determine who we should be, what and who we should love, and how we should live, we experience the outcomes of our own suppression in the form of anger, depression, stress, anxiety, addiction, exhaustion, or illness.

We cannot fully express our creative nature and consciously create our reality without giving ourselves the freedom to create what we truly want.

Fear and Control

Dealing with another person's right to choose his or her path in life according to his or her preferences and beliefs is a forceful act of control that nourishes the need for superiority.

Constant fights and long-standing grudges between parents and their children often result from the parent's insistence that he or she knows what's best for the child, even when the child is already a grown-up. If the parents asked themselves, "What does my child really need?" instead of, "What do I think is right for him or her?" they might find that often what they insist is good for the child causes him or her ongoing suffering.

A few years before passing away, my father went through a bypass procedure, and since he was a heavy smoker, the doctors strongly recommended he immediately quit. We, the family members, made a joint effort to prevent him from smoking, out of concern for his health. In the following years he had to smoke in secret and to ask his colleagues for cigarettes like a beggar. Today I understand how awful and pointless it was to ask him to give up the one thing that provided him with a sense of vitality and freedom, and how this act, instead of promoting his health, promoted his death at the relatively young age of seventy.

Many who are driven by fear invest huge amounts of energy in the attempt to control the people and the circumstances around them. They are always on guard in case what they fear happens; the wife forbids her husband from spending time with his friends lest he meets attractive women, and the husband criticizes his wife's clothing that might draw the attention of another man.

Manipulations—such as blaming, exploiting someone's guilty conscience, pushing him or her toward the "right" decision, or demonstrating disappointment and anger—force others to comply with our wishes. But despite the relief that we feel when we get what we want, we may feel guilty about our behavior, and frustrated that the other person's choice wasn't an act of free will.

The futile attempt to control the circumstances, the choices, and the reactions of those around us creates enormous pain and often ends in failure. The conflicts, the stress, and the constant fear that go along with it are the real sources of our misery, not what we dread might happen if only we loosen our grip.

Emotional Coercion

Emotional coercion comes from a burning desire for another person to accept our ways, agree with our opinions, and constantly prove his or her love to soothe our pain.

In romantic relationships, the fear of losing the love of a spouse may trigger obsessive behavior accompanied by endless demands that supposedly prove his or her love, such as the number of times he or she should call during the day, or a demand to demonstrate physical intimacy even when he or she doesn't feel like it. Difficulty to give others the space they need stems from a constant need for approval and inability to deal with what is perceived as rejection. Such a person cannot respect the wishes and needs of another if they don't match his or hers, just like a person who forces him- or herself on another.

A client of mine told me how her mother gave her a talking-to every time she was angry with her. These talks were kind of exhausting lectures in which the mother would mention all the mistakes the daughter ever made and blame her for not loving her enough. As a child my client hated this, yet had no choice but to sit and listen. As an adolescent she started fighting back, but it was equally exhausting and only triggered her mother's reaction. Only as an adult, when she learned how to be assertive with her mother, did she manage to put an end to it. Being forced to sit and listen to those reasonless lectures made her feel like she was being emotionally raped and evoked huge anger.

Often an unconscious person coerces those around to listen to his or her complaints and support his or her battle against a current enemy. If only they dare to express disagreement, they will swiftly become the unconscious person's enemies themselves.

From Controlling Others to Self-Control

Despite the understanding of how wrong their actions are, fearful people who cannot give space to others feel at the moment of truth that they simply can't control themselves. They fail to resist the urge to check what's going on, and when they surrender to it, they become even more anxious.

How is it possible, then, to develop self-control?

Getting out of our heads—Before we become present and learn to identify the patterns of fear-based thinking while they happen, we see reality through a veil of painful thoughts driven by a fear of rejection. Often I speak to women who cannot see the love of their partner. In their minds, the sole purpose of their partner's words and actions is to get them into bed or to keep them around in order to fill the void in his life. Such a woman finds it hard to resist spying on her partner, feels hurt when she believes her thoughts and therefore keeps picking fights and can't enjoy the relationship. When, following her behavior, a distance is created between her and her partner, she sees it as proof of her suspicions. If she would have questioned her thoughts, the imaginary scenarios may still run through her head but she wouldn't react to them as if they were true. Instead, she would look into her partner's eyes, feel his touch, and sense the emotions behind his words in order to know what he really feels.

Embracing uncertainty—When we are swamped with fear, there is an almost uncontrollable impulse to find what's going on. After a breakup, many struggle with the thought that their former partner will win an imaginary race by finding a new relationship before they do, and thus they monitor his or her online activity to make sure they can stay calm. Those who surrender to the urge to know someone's whereabouts straightaway, or to get an immediate response from him or her, text or call obsessively, stressing themselves out and imposing a burden on the other person. Such actions relieve the tension, but in the long run they amplify it many times over. "But I can't stand not knowing!" some might say. Yet it's only when we are not giving in to the impulse to check what's going on that it subsides, and over time the ability to remain calm in the face of uncertainty becomes second nature.

Giving up drama and negativity—Over time I have learned that the thing that most affects emotional imbalance, and thus self-control, is emotional drama. How come? Emotional drama—self-pity, self-blame, blaming others, and complaining—turns an unpleasant situation into something we can't deal with. It weakens the body and the soul, and as a result, at the moment of truth we have no power left to deal with the situation, and all we long for is a moment of relief.

Freedom

I have found that it's only when I have true freedom that I can be at ease, as I know I can change my decision anytime and be true to my heart.

A few years ago, I decided to drastically reduce the amount of refined sugars I consume. Prior to this decision I was a fan of sweets and never believed I could give them up. Still, it's easy for me to uphold my decision because I give myself full permission to change it at any time.

If we won't give ourselves permission to change our minds about crucial decisions, such as marriage, we'll immediately feel suffocated and find ourselves looking for our partner's faults in order to justify the necessity to do so.

When someone gives us space, we find ourselves drawn to his or her company; when he or she restricts us, always taking things personally, and is never satisfied with anything we do, we find ourselves withdrawing from him or her.

The ability to give ourselves and others the gift of freedom comes from understanding the importance of free will and the negativity that infects any action that does not stem from it. It doesn't mean that a child shouldn't be obliged to brush his or her teeth or tidy up his or her room; it means that there is no point in holding onto someone who wants to leave, or in forcing someone to avoid a friendship with another to prove his or her love to us.

Impeccability

When I think of the kind of person I want to see in front of me, I think of someone whose behavior is pleasant and respectful no matter the circumstances; who can manage his or her emotions, who shows genuine interest in others, who can stand in another person's shoes, who doesn't complain or hold grudges, who doesn't speak ill of others, and who knows how to assert him- or herself without being aggressive. We all want those around us to be like that, we look up to such people and blame others for lacking these qualities, but we always have plenty of justifications for not being like that ourselves.

When we understand that the key to freedom and peace of mind is to align our lives with what we talk about and what we expect of others, the passion to be as impeccable as we can with our way of being becomes a focal point.

Impeccability is the understanding that any word and action, no matter how negligible it seems, has an immediate impact on our feelings and our world. From this place it becomes easy to give up negativity—complaining, blaming, self-pity, being inconsiderate with the excuse we're having a hard time, belittling and offending others—as it's clear to us that those are the things that perpetuate the pain and the struggle in our lives.

It's the realization that as long as we haven't healed our family relationships, any action we take is contaminated with negative energy. Many try to achieve greatness and leave a mark in the world, but there is no real power in their achievements as long as they don't heal themselves and their homes, and sometimes only they know that despite everything they don't feel they are worthy.

Impeccability is not about being perfect or never making a mistake; there will always be human errors, but instead of using them as a reason for self-judgment, they now serve for learning.

The passion to reach impeccability and the joy it creates conclude this long chapter—at the point where we fully understand our role as the creators of our lives and are ready to take full responsibility for our creation.

PART FOUR

Creation and Fulfillment

Chapter 8

Changing from the Outside In

There's a paradox in the name of this chapter, as any lasting change starts from the inside out. And yet this chapter talks about creating a change from the outside in—as the internal creates the external, but the external perpetuates the internal.

Laying the Groundwork for Change

Before trying to make changes in our lives, we should look for the external conditions and behavioral patterns that maintain our inner state, for example:

- Many adults choose to live with their parents, even though the relationships are unhealthy, and while enjoying financial security they are exposed daily to energy full of negativity, to the source of their pain.
- A woman who's trying to love herself won't succeed as long as she's proving herself, through relationships with physically or emotionally unavailable, offensive, or abusive men, that if she won't settle for substitutes for

love, she'll have nothing.
- A person who demands constant validation about being worthy or loved, although gaining some relief in the short-term, becomes addicted to it, and thus even more insecure when he or she doesn't get it.
- Someone who patronizes others, disciplines, gives constant advice, and disrespects or humiliates others, enjoys a momentary burst of superiority, but at the same time such acts deepen his or her sense of worthlessness.
- When we ask for constant advice, we learn to believe that we can't make wise decisions on our own.
- We cannot let go of resentment toward our life partners before we learn to set boundaries with them and accept them wholeheartedly, along with the flaws they are unable to change.
- It's not possible to overcome food preoccupation as long as we treat food as an enemy, starve our bodies, or deny ourselves the foods we love most.
- And it's not possible to let go of fear as long as our decisions are driven by it.

The attempt to control our thoughts, emotions, and reactions before changing the external aspects that maintain our inner state, is the main reason for the frustrating gap between knowing and doing that many experience.

Only when we dare to change what we cannot accept and give up destructive behavioral patterns that provide short-term satisfaction is change initiated.

Why Are People Treating Me This Way?

When we realize that the world is a mirror and that we are responsible, through our attitude, behavior, and emotions, for the way people treat us, we can start to examine our surroundings to understand what we are creating.

Often we are like the giant who shakes the dwarf's hand. "Gently, please," asks the dwarf. "But it was extremely gentle," answers the giant, oblivious to the fact that even his most delicate handshake can break the dwarf's hand.

When someone says, "You are like this or like that…," the pain that we feel might upstage our ability to listen, and immediately we begin to justify ourselves and blame the other person for what he or she dared to say. But even if from our point of view the other person's words don't make any sense, it may help, before we dismiss them out of hand, to try to understand what was the impact of our actions on him or her and what made him or her say these words.

Sometimes a client complains about the negative attitude of her mother toward her. When I ask if her mother ever said that she feels judged and rejected by her, my client admits that. Yet, upon my client's judgment, there is no place for her mother's feelings, as the mother is supposed to be the "adult". Instead of trying to understand how she hurts her mother—which is what leads to her mother's aggressive reaction—she childishly insists that her mother shouldn't be so childish and start acting like an adult.

When a certain feedback comes up again and again, we may want to check the reason for it. If at any workplace we find ourselves in the middle of a conflict, we may choose to believe it's because of the problematic nature of those around us or jealousy of our success, though the question of why we in particular get this attitude remains unanswered. Because if you look into it, you will find that those difficult people are not getting into fights with everyone, and that not every successful person is being tripped.

Knowing that I'm fully responsible for the reality I'm creating, I examine my impact on everything, and especially on the relationships in which I'm involved, and every time I ask myself, "What was my impact on the situation?" and, "How did I create that?" even if the situation was not fully in my control. Several times when the tempers flared at a family gathering, I understood that it happened because I lost my cool. Although I wasn't the only one responsible, when I was "weighing anchor" too, the ship started sinking. When I take responsibility for my impact, I can make sure that such a situation won't happen again, as the price all participants pay is too high.

How Do Words Create Reality?

Our way of expression accurately reflects what's going on inside of us—our beliefs, expectations, and real feelings. Not necessarily the words we pronounce but the way we articulate ourselves; the intonation, facial expressions, and body language that accompany the words.

When someone denies the truth, the way he articulates his words always reveal his (or her) true feelings. "I'm not angry with her anymore," a client declares. "So why do you look as if you've just bitten into a lemon?" I ask. Often people are quick to say, "No, I'm not angry at all," while their faces are twisted with contempt. Their facial expressions are meant to emphasize the inferiority of the person toward whom they supposedly feel no anger.

Our words and the way we express them, what we say and what we avoid saying, have an enormous influence on the reality we create and on the toxic negativity inside us. Curiosity for our words and for the feelings that arise in us following their expression can teach us about the limiting beliefs that run our lives, about unconscious fears, about grudges we're still holding, and about unrealistic expectations we are not willing to give up.

When someone says, "I hope," the true meaning of the words is, "I want it, but I don't believe I can achieve it." When he or she dares to declare, "I've decided," or, "I intend to," he or she immediately straightens up from within.

Being aware of the way we express ourselves is an effective way to jump-start a desired change. We can't always control our thoughts, and our beliefs can't be changed with a simple decision; but we have, with some attention, almost full control over the way we express ourselves.

Speaking Positively

Many theories have been written about the idea that our thoughts and words shape our reality. But I'd like to question a misguided belief that stems from the positive thinking genre—that if we think positively, everything will be positive. Or more accurately, as most people interpret it, that if we say we think positively, everything will be positive.

A thought is a bunch of words that in themselves have little effect on our reality. It's the emotions that hide beneath our words that affect our creation. Almost anything can be said in a positive or negative context, from a fearful or peaceful place. The sentence "I probably won't get married" might send a shiver down one's spine, whereas for another it's simply stating a fact, just like saying, "The weather is nice today."

The positive thinking genre doesn't serve its purpose, because the positive words are being used too quickly, in an attempt to sweep the "negative" emotions—disappointment, frustration, or fear—under the rug. When we use it, we may be quick to suppress natural emotions, and as a result, fail to bridge the gap between mind and heart.

Venting

Venting—what's also called blowing off steam or getting things off our chests—is perceived as a healthy, stress-relieving activity that allows us to express emotions that will blow up inside us if we don't speak them. Is that so? Intuitively it seems to be right. When we share our feelings with another person and "get them off our chests," we feel better for a while. Still, the terms "venting" and "releasing" are misleading. This so-called "release mechanism" is essentially a conversation full of complaints, blame, self-justification, and victimhood, in which we use harsh and even violent words toward a third party, while overlooking our part in the situation and expecting others to blindly agree with us and do whatever they can to convince us that everything will be okay.

"My ex explained to me why I'm never going to have a long-term relationship," an emotional client says sobbing. Later, when she calms down, she asks me what she should do in order to move forward. "To begin with, start taking responsibility for what comes out of your mouth," I reply. "When you insist that the harmful words of your ex-boyfriend are true, you deliberately treat the worst-case scenario as a fact, whereas at the present moment anything is possible."

"Right," she admits, "and not only was I crying to you about it, but also to my mother, to my friends, and even to my boss."

"And what were you trying to achieve?" I ask. "I wanted people to calm me down, to say that I'm young and beautiful and that everything will be all right," she answers with a devious smile.

Eventually, not only did her attempts to "milk" encouragement not ease the pain, but dwelling on the subject increased her identification with the painful thoughts.

Talking incessantly about our problems, about other people, and about how we've been wronged, doesn't relieve anything. On the contrary, it intensifies our pain, justifies our grudges and sense of victimhood, and strengthens feelings of despair. And what for? "Venting," just like scratching, provides momentary relief, but at the same time it prevents healing and leaves ugly scars. The longed-for relief it provides quickly disappears, but the negative energy it creates keeps living within us for a long time.

"Isn't it worse to keep your emotions locked up inside?" you may ask. What we express aloud is merely a reflection of what's going on within us. Thus, when someone is not ready to give up the self-enhancement gained by complaining and blaming, and the attention self-pity invites, he finds it hard to take responsibility for his (or her) words. A conscious person, who understands how by "venting" he actually magnifies the pain and hurts himself, can stop for a moment and notice his actions: "I'm blaming again," or, "I'm pitying myself again." If following such observation he still feels the need to get support and share his (or her) feelings, there's nothing wrong with that. Let's go back to my heartbroken client for a moment. She may still choose to share her feelings without unnecessary drama: "I miss him," "I'm angry," "I feel fear." Personally, I find that the inner peace created through presence practice helps me more than anything to get back on my feet and find the answers within.

Emotional Vampires

"Emotional vampire" is an appropriate nickname for someone who, under a cover of goodwill, feeds off the misery of others. Following a conversation with such a person, after getting plenty of advice and hearing astonishing stories about him or her, you will find that you said things you didn't want to, and that somehow you feel worse than before you "got the burden off your chest."

We may all feel slightly better about ourselves when we hear about the troubles of others, but such people have a compulsive need to feed off other people's misery and a miraculous ability to persuade others to pour their hearts out.

When we understand that such a "vampire" is standing in front of us, instead of blaming him or her for who he or she is, we can choose to limit our interaction with this person.

Dramatization

Sometimes we may find ourselves building a sad and dramatic story around the circumstances to emphasize our misery and justify our choices and accusations. For example:

- "My children will be better off if I commit suicide," a client declares dramatically. When I'm asking her to stand in their shoes for a moment and check this statement from their perspective, she admits she exaggerated.
- When a daughter says about her father, "He's not a father like the world intended," there's a whole drama behind her

statement, which may sound like this: Everyone but me has a normal father, and thus the situation is terrible and I deserve pity.
- "I can't live without sex," a beautiful divorced mother in a respected profession justifies her reluctance to let go of the unavailable men that fill her spare time. "It's the only spot of light in my life," she adds and starts crying.
- Harsh statements, such as, "I'm dead inside," "My life is a living hell," or, "I can't take it anymore," accompanied by dramatic intonation and crying, intensify the pain, and drain the energy required to effectively deal with the situation.

Despite the pain it creates, dramatization is an addictive habit, and when we turn every little thing into a drama, the question is how will we respond when we are faced with a real challenge.

The story behind the words hides internal resistance to *what is* and implies that everything should, and could have been different. If you pay attention to the feelings that arise when you repeat the dramatic story, you will find that most of your pain is not due to circumstances but to the sad story you insist on adding to them.

Labeling Yourself

When someone repeatedly says, "I'm like this and like that…" it becomes a part of his or her identity. A woman who's labeling herself as lazy is not describing a personality trait but treating herself in an offensive way, sometimes due to criticism she has received in the past. Such an expression disregards personal temperament, emotional state, or preferences. It's not forgiving toward the need for rest and recovery, and has only one purpose—to hurt oneself.

"I never dare to." "I always fail." Such statements, even if accurately reflecting all we have experienced so far, also determine that the rest of our lives will look the same. Instead we can say, "Up until today I was such and such…, and now I choose to…," or simply add nothing. The important part is letting go of the assumption hiding behind such statements—that whatever happened in the past will necessarily happen in the future, and that we have no choice about it.

Once you stop complaining that you don't believe that something you want will come true in your life, the belief that it's possible immediately strengthens, and only when you let go of the labels you have put on yourself can you become the person you want to be.

Accuracy

Often our words stand in our way and turn a simple change into something that seems beyond reach. "The relationship is not his first priority," says a client, accusing her partner. When we get to the bottom of it, she understands that she is often impatient with him and rejects his initiatives. Her reactions affect his motivation and push him away, yet her words make her feel as if she is the victim. "I want my partner to be stronger than me," says a friend, describing her ideal partner. But what exactly is she looking for? What defines a strong person? Is it that he tends to suppress his emotions where she's prone to drama? Is it that he overlooks his problems by constantly dealing with hers? Is it that he buries his feelings so deeply that his body expresses the pain through obesity or illness? And maybe his life looks perfect, but he still needs alcohol, narcotics, or psychiatric drugs to run away from his pain. Often when one of my clients describes her partner as strong, out of her words appears a man haunted by feelings of worthlessness that he is struggling to hide.

Expressions such as "living in the light" or "acting without ego" sound admirable, but at the moment of truth they provide no practical guidance and allow us to overlook the negativity we are still not willing to give up.

By using pretentious words and setting vague and unrealistic goals, we turn a simple change that can be implemented at the present moment into a grandiose goal that might be achieved one day with considerable effort. "I want to fully awaken," states a client. In practice she needs to be aware that she still blames her brother, and to stop feeling sorry for herself for being single. "I don't understand how to break the identification with the pain-body,"* complains another. In practice she needs to be aware of the unrealistic expectations she has of her mother, which make her angry and miserable.

Statements that conceal hidden meanings allow us to express negativity in disguise. The expression "It's sad," for instance, when referring to oneself, usually testifies to self-pity; when referring to another, it's often intended to present him or her as inferior to us and thus provide us with a sense of superiority. "I pity him," says a client about her ex-boyfriend who cheated on her. It's obvious that she has no compassion for him; instead, she takes pleasure in implying his weakness and failure.

---

* The pain-body—a terminology coined by spiritual teacher and author Eckhart Tolle—is an accumulation of old emotional pain that almost everyone carries in his or her energy field. When, through conscious presence, we break the identification with the thoughts related to the pain, it loses energy and no longer runs our internal dialogue.

When we strip our words from slogans, generalizations, and hidden meanings, they can help us touch the root of the problem, the painful aspect that stands in our way and affects our happiness.

The Amazing Power of Non-Reactivity

Reactivity is a communication pattern that resembles the exchange of verbal blows. This communication pattern is so deeply rooted in our culture that using it not only seems inevitable, but is often justified by statements such as, "I don't want to be a sucker," or "But she deserved it!" Non-reactivity, on the other hand, is a miraculous key for creating internal serenity as well as profound and immediate transformation in any relationship.

In order to understand what non-reactivity is, we should first understand what it is not. Non-reactivity is not non-reaction, though sometimes the best reaction is not to react, and it's not to overlook something and keep smiling while toxic resentment is building inside us. It's also not exactly to "count to ten," though taking a moment before reacting might be helpful. Non-reactivity is a reaction that does not involve self-justification or an attempt to pay someone back or to hurt him or her.

Here are some common ways of reactivity:

- Finger-pointing—"You are responsible for this...." "No, you are!" "But you...." "And you...." And so on. The tones: aggressive and harsh.
- Getting things off our chests—Often we are encouraged to confront the people who hurt us in order to get things off our chests and release the painful burden. Such an

act may supply temporary relief but due to its nature, it might ultimately intensify our negative emotions. The intent of the harsh words we tend to use in this context is not to work things out but to make the other person feel how awful he or she is, to offend, and to hurt, and by pronouncing them we automatically strengthen our victim identity. Usually we have such conversations with our parents and ex-partners. Our parents may easily feel guilty, even if they defend themselves and deny what we say. But what for? Would it make them change their ways? And how can they redeem the past? Our ex-partners usually have no interest in our opinions, and thus what's left is a futile attempt of a wounded ego to balance the insult it has experienced. The effective way to release the painful burden is not to put the blame on others, but to let go of it and set clear boundaries where they are needed.

- Defensiveness—Self-justification and exaggerated apologies intended to prove why I'm not to blame, why you didn't understand me correctly, and why you have to forgive me. The tones: self-justifying and whining.
- Counterattack—Often when people feel attacked or guilty, they are quick to strike back, whether or not they did something wrong. The tones: offended and self-righteous.
- Belittling others—Reactions such as, "Calm down," expressed in a cold and patronizing manner, are offensive reactions that are meant to make the other person feel stupid and small. When people describe an argument they've been involved in and say, "At least I stayed calm," it's not calmness they are talking about, but lack of compassion toward the other person's feelings, and contempt toward his or her struggle to control them.

Contrary to real calmness that involves no judgment, here the judgmental energy, which is felt even without words, triggers the other person's reaction.

- Giving a cold shoulder and stonewalling are forms of reactivity that send a message without words. "I'm hurt and angry," "You should redeem yourself," or, "You are not important enough for me to look up from my phone."
- Using meaningful facial expressions and body language, such as an eye-roll, which means, "Here she goes again," tight mouth, eyebrow raise, and a head-shake that mean, "You can't even do this properly."
- And more—Door slamming ("Keep talking to the walls!"), "I'm fine" ("Keep trying to appease me").

When we are in a reactive mood, we are not really interested in what the other person has to say or in his or her feelings. All we care about is to change a negative perception of us or to fend off irritating behavior. There is no dialogue, care, or friendship. The argument can go on and on and on, and even if eventually the parties reach an understanding, the emotional residue created in the process won't dissipate so fast.

Non-reactivity becomes possible only when we realize that our need to be right and obtain consent is keeping us away from our goals. Using it does not mean that nothing affects our feelings anymore, but that we consciously choose how to react to our inner drama because we understand the consequences of our actions. Regardless of how reactive the other person is, non-reactivity can turn things upside down in a way that leaves him or her puzzled and disarm him or her within seconds. Even if we have already fallen into reactivity, it's not too late to get a hold of ourselves and transform the situation by using non-reactivity.

A non-reactive reaction will be expressed in a practical

manner; in a rather neutral voice, without dramatic facial expressions and dismissive body language, and without defending ourselves or blaming the other person. Instead of dealing with the futile question, "Why?" we'll ask the magical question, "What can we do now?" And if an apology is needed, we'll give up defending ourselves and making empty promises, and simply acknowledge the other person's feelings by saying something like, "I'm sorry I made you feel that way."

The miraculous power concealed in non-reactivity was revealed to me during the leadership program I attended. One of the assignments we were given was to deliver a workshop in pairs. After the workshop I'd delivered with my partner, tension was built between us, and it escalated until we no longer spoke to each other. When, at the beginning of the next quarterly gathering of the group, we were asked to sit down in pairs to discuss the workshop we'd delivered, my partner declared in front of the whole group, "I'm not sitting with Sharon, not even for ten minutes." Some tried to convince her that despite being right, her refusal was hurting the entire group and that it was only ten minutes—but to no avail.

Although I felt anger, shame, and a strong impulse to justify myself, I remained still and listened. Eventually, I began to hear what she was really saying (as when we are in a reactive mood we interpret everything distortedly). I realized that she was actually saying, "Sharon doesn't love me and doesn't want me, and I'm not willing to be rejected again." Only then, I reacted and said, "From my point of view it looks the same. Until yesterday I, too, felt angry with you and blamed you for the way you treated me. When you feel like it, you are welcome to talk to me." Later that day she gave me feedback in a group exercise, the day after, she invited me to have lunch together, and by evening we surprised the entire group when we put up a show at the talent night, even before they knew we'd made up.

It's hard to put into words the feelings associated with that event—pride in my behavior, wonder about the sequence of events, joy, serenity, and a deep sense of connection to who I really am.

What made it possible for me to do what I had dreamed of for so long but never managed before—to avoid a harsh reaction that would later make me feel sorry—was the inner peace I have found at the time through presence practice, and the understanding that through my reactions I was the one creating the situation I often complained about—that people didn't like me. Since then I'm using non-reactivity frequently, and every single time I'm surprised and amazed by its effectiveness.

The Simplest Way to Get the Attitude You Wish For

We all teach those around us how to treat us, but often we do it unconsciously. We operate within a certain framework of standards that teaches others about our boundaries, we say what we expect of them but allow the exact opposite, or we easily give in to their wishes and demands.

The fundamental flaw in the teaching method we use with fellow humans is that it relies on words instead of actions ("But what can I do? No matter how many times I try to explain, nothing happens!").

Reality proves that people, just like animals, learn only through actions; empty threats teach those around us that our words shouldn't be taken seriously. If I'm "running" after someone who's expressing anger or sadness in order to get attention, I'm teaching him or her that manipulations pay. Giving in to a child upon the excuse that the drama he or she might create isn't worth the fight, teaches the child it's worth creating a drama to achieve his or her goals. And when the employee complains that the tasks she was given are above her capacity yet stays late at work to complete them, she teaches her boss that despite her frustration she is the best candidate for the next task.

Setting Personal Boundaries

Due to the fear of anger and the continuous attempt to be "good" in order not to experience rejection, we are constantly shifting between submissiveness and aggressiveness, and find it difficult to set effective boundaries. Those who tend toward submissiveness pay a high price when they repeatedly suppress their anger, and those who tend toward aggressiveness pay a price, too, when by being aggressive they are intensifying their anger and inviting a harsh counter-reaction.

Effective boundary-setting includes the following steps:

1. Defining your boundaries—Boundaries are a personal matter that should reflect your preferences and needs. Sometimes you know what boundaries you need to establish to feel comfortable; at other times your actions teach you what's right for you through your emotional reaction to circumstances.

2. Defining the outcomes of crossing them—Once you have decided what boundaries you want to set, you need to determine the outcomes of crossing them. It cannot be an

empty threat such as, "If you do that, I'll be really angry with you," or a meaningless statement such as, "That's absolutely unacceptable!" It must be something concrete you are willing to stand wholeheartedly behind. Empty words will only teach the other side that he can keep doing what he wants, as at most he (or she) will have to bear some complaining and yelling.

3. Setting your boundaries—When you establish a new boundary, you should first explain your decision and the expected outcomes of not respecting it. It should be done in a calm manner, without apology or blame, as if you were a traffic cop raising a stop sign. Boundary-setting is usually bound with changing a status quo; thus, if you do it without prior notice, in a moment of anger, it will be perceived as unfairness on the other side. Claims such as, "For twenty years I've been doing everything for you," or, "Enough, it can't go on like this anymore," won't lessen the sense of injustice the other person experiences. The same metaphorical stop sign could be raised in events that do not require the entire process, in which it's necessary to clarify to the other side, "That's it!" or, "This is out of bounds." Many parents, for instance, insist on "helping" their grown-up children establish a relationship, discipline their own children, or manage their finances, while their children try to talk them out of it in any possible way—with reason, with tears, or with anger—but the parents won't budge. What's required at such moments is to assertively say to the parent something like, "I'm not going to discuss it anymore," and if the parent goes on, to add, "If you keep talking about it, I won't answer." Then to stand by your words. If you try to set boundaries with your parents, but then you run to them every time you

need reassurance, don't be surprised if they don't respect your boundaries.

4. Maintaining your boundaries—When you deny someone a benefit he or she was regularly given, you should expect resistance in the form of anger, blame, rebellion, or crying. At this point, you should stand firm behind your decision until the spirits calm down. Since it might be challenging, it is important that the rationale behind your actions is clear to you.

It's not the technique, however, that really matters, but the answer to the question, "If it's so simple, why doesn't it work at the moment of truth?" Most of us fail to set boundaries not due to lack of knowledge, but due to conflicting motives that influence our decisions, including:

Unwillingness to pay the price—It's perfectly fine to decide that the possible outcome of setting boundaries might be too high—that I'm not willing to hear the "no" my partner might say if I won't compromise on the attitude I expect, or that I'm not ready to quit my job if I don't get the promotion I've asked for. Many avoid taking action yet keep complaining about the situation, unwilling, either, to accept it as it is.

Unwillingness to fully understand the situation—We often refuse to come to terms with the other person's level of consciousness and thus, with his or her ability to change, and pointlessly complain, "I told him how much it hurts me, so I expect him to consider my feelings!" Instead of accepting the situation and setting our boundaries accordingly, we fill ourselves with negative energy through our repeated complaints and internal resistance to the circumstances.

Internal conflicts—A mother may find herself struggling

with setting boundaries for her child because she needs him or her to keep being her baby, she pities the child or is afraid to lose the child's love. And a woman who's looking for a committed relationship may find it difficult to give up the momentary comfort offered by a man who's only looking for a casual relationship.

Childhood fears, superstitions, and false perceptions— Childhood fears, such as fear of rejection, or superstitions, as the fear that something bad will happen to someone close to us because we didn't comply with his or her wishes, may unconsciously drive our decisions. Outdated social conventions and fictitious perceptions, such as "the good person who is never angry" or "the good wife who does everything for her husband," may lead us to ignore the inner voice that reminds us of our boundaries and instead judge ourselves for our feelings and reactions.

Boundary-Setting, Negativity, Tolerance, and Compassion

Many mistakenly think that enlightened people accept any person under any circumstances, are never angry, and are always compassionate and understanding.

Though compassion is essential for a life of happiness and choice, it doesn't mean that we have to accept everything with patience. Eventually, even after we've practiced non-reactivity, created boundaries, and given up our grudges, an unconscious person will continue to behave in an offensive way from time to time, simply because the negative energy within him or her needs an outlet. Thus, despite being compassionate and understanding, when we start to awaken, we have to take responsibility for the nature of our relationships. When dealing with relationships that cannot be cut off, or it is not recommended to do so, such as working relationships or close family, we need to use non-reactivity and to set clear boundaries in order to avoid further harm. When it comes to relationships of choice, such as romantic relationships or friendships, that make us feel used, or involve disrespect or lack of interest in us, sometimes the best choice is to end the relationship instead of holding on to it out of fear.

When you are too lenient with difficult people because you buy into their sad stories, you are not necessarily helping them. Before I awakened, I used to stick with those who were tolerant of me and in a way I "sucked their blood." But it was those who didn't accept my behavior, didn't let me cling to them, and insisted I was capable who helped me overcome my destructive behavioral patterns, not the ones who protected me and treated me like a child who was allowed everything.

Sweet Boundary-Setting

Sweet boundary-setting is the healthy and satisfying substitute for "sweet revenge"—the destructive behavioral pattern that provides short-lived satisfaction but at the same time intensifies negativity and pain.

When we ask someone to change his or her ways, our words have little effect, even if we explain ourselves clearly. But when we dare to set clear boundaries, the other person is left puzzled, and all that is left for him or her is to change his or her ways or leave. What leaves the other person puzzled are the calmness and decisiveness in which we express ourselves.

When we respect ourselves and our boundaries, we

prevent ourselves from getting into situations where someone has hurt us so much that we cannot resist the urge for revenge.

∴

At this point I find myself wondering about further examples that explain how to implement boundary-setting and how to react in any given situation, yet I understand that this is the exact opposite of what you need. I want to remind you that when you seek advice, you lose touch with your inner source of power, and to assure you that when you are present and calm, you will know exactly what to do and it will be done in the most loving and respectful way.

Supporting the Process of Change

Vitamins, better food, medical attention, may temporarily rejuvenate the body, but unless you change your beliefs it will quickly become swamped again by your feelings of depression.
    ~ Jane Roberts, The Nature of Personal Reality. A Seth Book

The tools I will shortly present may not solve the root cause of your problems, but they supply essential support to any process of personal growth and transformation, and to a large extent are vital to its success.

Physical Activity

Regular physical activity is necessary for emotional and physical health. It is vital for children's development and health, and may be used as a tool through which the child learns to trust him- or herself and release tension. Many tend to avoid physical activity once they feel bad or in pain, but often pain and lack of energy are the result of lack of activity, and in times of illness, releasing the stiffness accumulated in the body promotes healing. And how will you know how much physical activity you need? Simply by listening to your body.

Healthy Nutrition

When we become present and still, the ability to listen to the body's needs sharpens, our diet becomes healthier, and we prefer fresh and vital foods. Today there's plenty of available information through which anyone can educate him- or herself about nutrient-rich foods and about balancing weight without a diet. I'm not ruling out professional guidance, but as an experienced yo-yo dieter, I don't recommend a preordained diet regimen, because no one besides you can know what foods are right for you, what your optimal eating hours are, the quantities suitable for your body, and the balance between unhealthy (but loved) and healthy foods that will free you from overly thinking about food and diets.

Manual Healing Treatments

Emotional and physical stress can affect the body and lead to exhaustion and fatigue. At such times, manual healing treatments, such as massage, acupuncture, and shiatsu, can soothe the body and promote healing processes.

Chapter 9

Reality Creation

A lot has been said about what's called "reality creation"—the ability to make our wishes come true. Books have been written, formulas presented, and millions have been spent in order to reveal the secret. But despite the truth in all that's been said, most teachings overlook the dilemma of lack of control, i.e., the answer to the question of why it is so challenging to be positive, to love ourselves, and to believe that what we want is possible for us. That's why I've spent the majority of this book describing in detail all the factors that create fear, negativity, and lack of control. Without a deep understanding of those, conscious creation is not possible.

The final chapter of the book talks about the wondrous world that lies beyond negativity and lack of control, a world in which what's possible exceeds what we could ever imagine.

Preparing for Success

Just before you start pursuing your dreams, it will be wise to examine what brought you the wanted and unwanted outcomes you achieved so far, to "hoe" and "plow" the internal ground.

Why Is This Happening to Me?

Through a genuine attempt to figure out the answer to the question, "Why is this happening to me?" we can discover why the results we are getting don't match our expectations. A close examination will probably reveal that what happens in our lives accurately reflects our expectations. Not necessarily what we wish for but what we see in our mind's eye—often what we fear.

After one too many heartbreaks, I was sitting with myself to conduct a serious introspection. When I was looking into the possible reasons for the miserable outcome I achieved, I figured a couple of things. Before meeting the guy who broke my heart I had a general vision of the man suitable for me but I hardly ever managed to hold it in my mind. When I was seriously thinking about a relationship with such a person it seemed a bit boring to me, and my words would often draw a future of loneliness. Before leaving for the vacation where I met that guy, I pictured myself having a good time with an attractive man—and this is exactly what happened.

Until this point I used to think of myself as unlucky in relationships, in contrast to other areas of my life. When I examined my expectations, however, I realized that the same way I always got the job I dreamed of, I have more than once achieved the exact relationship I was aiming for. My beliefs regarding what's possible for me were the reason that my creation was bound with disappointment.

Surrendering to What Is

When the driving force for pursuing our goals is inner resistance to *what is*, we treat the current situation as an enemy that should be defeated—our weight, family status, or anything else—and thus, we are haunted by fear; the fear that we won't achieve the thing that is supposed to save us from suffering, and that the achievement won't bring the desired satisfaction, as suggested by past experience.

From a place of resistance, our actions often become ineffective, and we struggle for years to achieve our goals without success, or we might pursue our goals no matter what, without considering the quality of the outcomes. When the goal is to get married, we sometimes forget to consider what everyday life will be like with our chosen one; when the goal is X lb/kg in Y amount of time, we often overlook the way the diet affects our mood and threatens our health, and we ignore the prior knowledge that such a diet will probably end in failure again.

Surrendering to *what is* does not mean giving up; it's the understanding that the ongoing misery we create with our own hands is too much, and that the way we act only keeps us away from our goals.

At the age of twenty-three, I managed to overcome the eating disorder I'd suffered from for eight years by then. It was when one morning I woke up with a clear understanding: "Even if I'll carry some extra weight for the rest of life, it's not worth the suffering involved in thinking about food all day, every day." I realized that the price I was paying in pursuing my goal was too high. "I'll never diet again!" I said to myself. It's hard to describe the relief that followed this decision—it felt like someone removed ten tons from my shoulders in one fell swoop. And what happened after this morning? I adopted a balanced eating style that included healthy foods, as well as self-permission to enjoy the unhealthy foods I love on a daily basis, with attention to quantities and forgiveness for occasional overeating. Through the willingness to surrender to my life circumstances I achieved immediate and absolute freedom from eating disorders, and within a year I also reached my goal weight without effort.

When we bring acceptance into a certain situation, all we need to accept is the present moment, not the "fact" that it will always be like that (which is, of course, not surrendering to *what is* but complaining about a possible future).

Who Should You Be in Order to Have What You Want?

As you eradicate toxicity from your energy fields, you clean the ethers and attract other energy to yourselves, energy that vibrates with love. Like attracts like.
  ~ Barbara Marciniak, Family of Light

Do you know those couples that when you look at them you are thinking, "It's clear why they are together," as there is something similar in their personal qualities that explains why they were drawn to each other? Do you know those employees whose leadership potential shows at first sight? Those who often possess a kind of inner wholeness atypical of our culture despite their young age?

We may be easily filled with bitterness when not getting what we believe we deserve, when despite our skills someone else gets the promotion again, or when we are being treated unfairly. We believe that when things finally work out, the satisfaction we feel will make it possible for us to become who we want to be. But since the world can only reflect what's inside us, the way to achieve what we want is to become the person we believe we would be had we already achieved what we desire. Thus, if you want a mature and compassionate partner by your side, you should be like this yourself; if you want your boss to see you as worthy of promotion, you should first be the person whose conduct justifies the promotion; and if you want your children to respect you, you should first respect them and yourself. The real meaning of the sentence, "Act as if you already have it," is not only to imagine your dream partner waiting for you at home, but also to be the person you believe you would be if you had the relationship you are after.

Therefore, the most important part in creating our reality and fulfilling our dreams, the part that is often neglected, is the answer to the questions, "Who should I be, moment by moment, to attract that person/thing into my life?" and, "What are the things that I'm still allowing myself that create the opposite of what I want?"

Letting Go of Limiting Beliefs

You are given the gift of the gods; you create your reality according to your beliefs; yours is the creative energy that makes your world; there are no limitations to the self except those you believe in.
~ Jane Roberts, The Nature of Personal Reality. A Seth Book

Reality is a mirror of our beliefs, of our limiting beliefs as well as of our inner knowing of the infinite possibilities life offers. When we believe that something doesn't exist, even if it's in front of us, we do not see it: a loving attitude toward us, the genuine interest another person shows in us, or our good looks.

Beliefs that are deeply entrenched within a certain culture may influence the individual profoundly—when someone believes that at a certain age he or she is supposed to feel or function in a certain way, his or her body responds to it unconsciously, like being under suggestion. Similarly, when someone doesn't buy into the accepted belief systems, his or her body responds accordingly.

When I got free of the eating disorder I'd suffered from, I decided that chocolate and ice cream were not fattening. "These foods are swiftly digested and leave the body in no time," was the rationale behind my assertion. And indeed, though these foods were part of my diet for years, I didn't feel heavy when eating them, and they didn't make me gain weight.

The way to let go of limiting beliefs is to accurately identify them and then to disprove our identification with them. When a limiting belief dissolves, the inner knowing within us unfolds in the form of intuitive understanding or a clear hunch that requires no evidence—the knowing that I deserve what I want, that I'm worthy as I am, that I don't have to prove anything.

Beliefs are not speculations or wishful thinking but fear- and-limitation-based perceptions of reality we have come to think of as true. At the root of our beliefs lie childhood and cultural conditioning that manifest as expectations (what we see in our mind's eye), assumptions that we perceive as facts ("Knowledge is power," "Women are more emotional than men"), or complaints we have repeated so many times, that we've forgotten they are not inevitable ("No one I like will ever like me back," "I will always be like this or like that…").

It's important, though, to understand that when something recurs in our lives, like difficulty to maintain steady relationships or recurring conflicts at work, it's not just an outcome of limiting beliefs, but also of behavioral patterns that we should change in order to get different results.

Create a list of your beliefs regarding a certain topic, such as relationships, career, or health. If the chosen topic is health, your beliefs may be around the following subjects: the connection between physical activity and health, between nutrition and health, between age and health, between heredity and health, the body's ability to cure itself, and the importance of regular health checkups.

To later question your beliefs, start with writing them down as personal, definitive statements. Instead of, "I believe there's a connection between heredity and heart disease," write, "It's only a matter of time until I'll get a heart attack, like all the men in my family," or, "My genetics suck." Instead of, "Most men cheat on their wives," write, "Men are natural-born cheaters; eventually, I'll be cheated on too." The most accurate wording will be the way things sound in your head without filtering, in moments of pain or late at night.

The following questions will assist you in identifying your beliefs:

- What are the scary scenarios running through your head regarding the future?
- What are the statements you express aloud or in your head regarding the selected topic?
- What offends you (as deep down you believe it is true)?
- What things do you avoid telling about yourself and maybe even lie about, such as age, marital status, or personal and professional history?
- What is something you did or didn't do that you believe stands in the way of your dream?

∴ And which contingency plans conceal the assumption that you are not going to fulfill your dream?

Read your list once a day for around two weeks, and ask yourself the following questions regarding each belief:

1. Does all the evidence, in my own life and in the lives of other people I know or have heard of, confirm this is the absolute truth?
2. If it happened before, will it necessarily happen again?
3. Though I see no evidence for it, could what I want still exist and come into my life?

(If you can't attribute any of these questions to a particular belief, you may need to rephrase it according to the above instructions.)

You might be reluctant to acknowledge your beliefs and think about them, lest they come true. But only by facing your beliefs can you break the identification with them and free yourself from the fear they create.

After the two-week process, keep paying attention to limiting beliefs that may still pop into your mind or express themselves in your words. At this stage, attention to your thoughts and words might be enough to break the identification with a limiting belief, and if needed, you can always write it down and go through this process for several days.

Breaking Free from Your "Personal Shell Shock"

"Personal shell shock" is a term I use to describe residual emotional pain from an event, or a number of childhood events, that served as proof that we were not good enough and caused a profound fear of rejection. At times this pain is dormant, but it can easily become active when an event that reminds us of the initial painful event happens. When the old pain arises, whether in reality or in a dream, we find ourselves awash in pain and rage.

"They are both cute, but the little one is cuter," was the statement burned in my mind, when at around eight, while my twin sister and I visited the library, I heard a teenage girl saying it to her friend. Even today I remember the shooting pain I felt when I heard those words. Throughout my childhood I've experienced the same pain under similar circumstances in a number of different events. As a consequence, over time I've developed a sound belief, that reality always mirrored faithfully, that I will never be a man's first choice.

It's important to understand, though, that the initial event is not the source of the pain, but only a mirror of the feelings of worthlessness and the limiting beliefs that already started to form during our early childhood, as a result of our parents' mental and emotional health and their attitudes toward us. Such a memorable event happens when we are old enough to analyze the situation and draw conclusions, usually between the ages of seven and nine, sometimes a bit earlier or later.

Some vividly remember the painful event; others only remember its essence. And there are those for whom significant parts of their childhood are shrouded in fog and thus they don't remember anything, or maybe they remember an event that might have caused pain but have no recollection of the feelings associated with it.

Whether you remember the initial event or not, what's important is to identify the painful scenario that reenacts itself again and again in your life, accompanied by burning pain and rage; it "assembles" the most suitable actors, "creates" the set that will enable the show, and in this way, it pushes you to acknowledge its existence and break free from its hold.

Breaking free is not so simple, yet it's certainly possible. Here are some steps that will assist you:

- The first step in breaking free from your personal shell shock is to clearly identify the pain it creates—look for the areas in which fear of rejection is running your life, and for the situations that make you feel like all you have achieved counts for nothing.
- When the old pain arises, acknowledge your feelings without judgment. Don't try to suppress or deny them. In order to break free from the pain, you will have to admit emotions that are considered a weakness, such as being jealous or hurt, instead of suppressing them and building resentment and hatred that produce a false sense of power.
- Should the painful scenario reappear in your life, you'll want to scream and wail about your bad luck. Instead, remain still and remember that the illusion can only dissolve when you recognize it for what it is—the same old drama that your mind continues to manifest.
- Any personal shell shock stems from a fear of rejection and therefore involves a constant effort to win recognition and love. As a consequence, it's always bound with self-disrespect, that is to say, with "selling ourselves short" for love. In order to let go of the pain, you must learn to respect yourself and set boundaries where needed, even when you fear losing the "love" you so desperately hold on to.
- Take responsibility for the times you are doing to others what's done to you while downplaying the significance of your actions. Since the world always teaches us about the consequences of our actions by demonstrating to us

how it feels on the other side, you'd have to stop doing to others what you don't want to experience yourself.
∴ And of course—use an extra dose of presence practice in order to stay calm in the midst of the storm and regain your strength.

∴

Breaking free from the grip of the personal shell shock is the final step of the awakening process, in which all we have learned should manifest—first we need to face our biggest fear without running away, then to take full responsibility for our attitude toward others, and eventually, to let go of the blame toward those who hurt us, toward the "actors" who answered our spiritual call and came to enact what still lives within us.

This is the final battle between the forces of light and the forces of darkness, a crucial battle in which fear is trying to overcome love. Whoever wins this battle gains true freedom.

The Birth of Events in Our Internal Reality

Each event we experience, just like a baby, develops first in our internal reality and only then shows up in the world. When we believe that something is impossible, we won't see it in our mind's eye (often we see the exact opposite), and it won't manifest in our lives. When no limiting beliefs stand in our way, what we wish for will manifest in our lives, often effortlessly.

To verify this assumption, I invite you to create a list and examine the nature of the desired events that have manifested in your life.

Below are some directions that will assist you:

- Think of something you really wanted and managed to achieve—a job you've longed for or someone you liked who later became your partner.
- A feeling of "dumb luck"—for example, your car broke down right next to the garage.
- Coincidences—a call from someone you'd thought about or a coincidental meeting with him or her.
- Times you found yourself doing something that later became useful, such as learning a foreign language that was required in a new job.
- Something that once seemed impossible and is now easy and natural, such as speaking in front of an audience or driving.
- Events of spontaneous healing or healing against all odds that you have experienced.
- Inner knowing that something that might have seemed unreasonable at the time was about to happen.
- Something you were determined to achieve and knew that nothing would stand in your way.

Some of the items in my list: a coincidental meeting with my former boss after thinking for a while about how much I want to thank him for the way he treated me, a coincidental meeting with someone I really wanted to meet at a time and a place that allowed us to sit comfortably and talk, several occasions of achieving the exact job I'd dreamed of, and a few times when books "jumped" right into my hands when I needed them most and had a tremendous impacted on my life. My list also includes things I have said about my personal and professional growth, even before fully understanding their meaning, which later turned out to be accurate, two occasions of spontaneous healing from severe hair loss, and decisions that the world simply obeyed at the moment I made them.

The most interesting thing about my list is something I've realized only after finishing it. Some of the statements that repeatedly show in my descriptions are, "I saw myself," "I knew it would happen," "I decided," "I was talking about it," and "I had a clear picture of it." Amazing, isn't it?

When you start your list, you may find it hard to recall the positive coincidences you have experienced, as we all tend to focus on what's not working. But don't give up; start with whatever you remember, even if it's just an event or two. When you start paying attention to such things, your awareness sharpens, and you automatically begin to notice new events and recall additional events from the past. Write everything down, even if it seems insignificant, as the process of manifestation is the same for what seems simple or complicated to you—it's only your beliefs that make it look that way.

Manifestation

The power of play was given to humans so they would be able to play with creation, gain experiences, have fun, and learn. "Be passionate and creative, and play as if everything is possible," God said "Aim to achieve your true desires, and if you fail, simply learn from it and create another game."

~ From "The Five Wondrous Powers"

The Creative Dynamics of Wanting

The meaning of the word "want" is simple if you ask a young child, but full of contradictions if you ask an adult. As a child, it was clear to you what you wanted and what you disliked.

Even today, if you are honest, it's clear to you, though today you often don't give permission to your true desires. The fear-based "need" and "must," which we mistakenly call wanting, became the driving forces behind our decisions.

Thus, before you look into ways to accomplish your goals, it's important that you provide yourself with an answer to the question, "What do I really want?" as this is what you will be given.

The process through which we manifest events in physical reality is simple:

1. A desire is born, either from love or fear.
2. We either have a sense of knowing that our desire is within our reach; or a limiting belief that it is not.
3. A mental image, composed of thought, interpretation, and emotion, forms a vision that we see in our mind's eye.
4. Eventually, a person, thing, or event comes into our lives, a three-dimensional manifestation that reflects our expectations.

Sometimes the desire is intense, yet the belief related to it is of lack and limitations, and accordingly, the manifested event is at best a dull substitute for what we have desired.

Anything that has enough energy, meaning there's a strong enough desire along with the inner knowing that it's possible, will manifest in our lives, whether it's driven by passion or by the need to prove our worth, by fear or by love. Some reach great achievements throughout their lives—prosperous careers, financial abundance, a loving family, and recognition—while driven by the need to prove they are worthy and loved, and constantly running away from the feeling of worthlessness that still haunts them.

The main difference between manifestations that come

from fear and manifestations that come from love is in their quality. Those "success stories," whose achievements are born of the need to prove their worth, will soon realize that their achievements can't fill the hole inside them—the road toward their goals won't be satisfying and no accomplishment will fill the emptiness.

Manifestation Toolkit

You get what you concentrate upon. There is no other main rule.
~ Jane Roberts, The Nature of Personal Reality. A Seth Book

The ability to manifest our desires in physical reality is based on the understanding that external reality is only a reflection of what's going on in our minds—of our beliefs, emotions, and expectations.

When no limiting beliefs stand in our way, the process of manifestation is effortless—we want something, see it in our mind's eye, pay attention to it, and sooner or later it manifests in our lives. The question is how can we change our perception when we have already experienced failure and disappointment and all we can imagine is more of the same.

Popular reality creation techniques provide a simple formula: focus on what you want instead of what you don't want, believe that it's possible for you, trust the universe to fulfill your wishes, express your gratitude for what's already in your life, and stay positive while working toward your goals. But despite the logic in this formula, many struggle to implement it. The difficulty is an outcome of the reign of fear and negativity; that's why the most important part of any fulfillment process is the shift from fear to love. When we give up negativity and fear releases its hold, a tremendous amount of energy that can be dedicated to focusing on our goals becomes available, and we automatically find it easier to believe we can have what we want.

Along with the manifestation techniques I will shortly present, don't forget to ground the greater part or your attention in the present moment. Using these techniques for a few minutes a day is enough to support the process. Note that you can't use them to control another person's free will or to hurt him or her.

Controlling our inner energy—Since our consciousness is the ground for what later manifests in our lives, the initial stage of any conscious manifestation is to become aware of what's inside us, of the thoughts and feelings arising within us moment by moment. It might sound complicated to track, but when we are still and present, no longer trying to run away from ourselves, we automatically become aware of them.

When you experience unwanted feelings or disturbing thoughts, don't try to avoid them. Instead, bring your attention back to the present moment. When we are present we are in harmony with *what is*, without inner resistance or fear. The present moment is the place where everything is possible—the place where disappointment about the past and fear of the future cannot run the show—and thus, it's the optimal starting point for creating a wanted reality.

Vision—Often when people are asked, "What do you want?" the answer is not clear to them. Most people know what they don't want, but like a ship sailing in the sea without a destination, it's not clear to them where are they navigating.

A vision has an added value only when our wishes are clear and limiting beliefs no longer stand in our way. When we are not sure what we want or we're trying to force ourselves to dedicate time to something our hearts are not into, the vision will be no more than a nice story.

A vision serves two purposes. One is to create clarity about the essence of what we want; the other is to answer the question, "Who am I, and how do I feel, react, and behave when my dreams are fulfilled?" and then to become this person now, in order to attract what we want into our lives

Many are afraid to be specific about their vision. "What if it makes me miss opportunities?" they ask. Because of this fear they eventually find themselves wasting precious time on something that had no chance of satisfying their heart's desire in the first place.

To understand why it's worth being accurate, go back to the list of things that you wanted and have achieved, and you will find that even before a certain event came true, you knew exactly what you wanted.

Write your vision as if it's occurring at the present moment or has occurred in the past (the event is taking place right now or has already happened), in as vivid, clear, and detailed as possible language. Read it once a day for about a month or until it becomes an integral part of your inner reality.

Mental rehearsal—The biggest secret to conscious manifestation is to fill yourself with the feeling that your prayer has already been answered.

Mental rehearsal is a powerful tool to support the creation of a wanted reality. It derives its inspiration from ancient traditions and is often used to improve performance in athletics or to support the development of other skills. It's all about deliberately using imagination and emotion to become one with what you want, as if your wish has already been fulfilled.

The following story, taken from an interview with the author Gregg Braden, demonstrates it well. "In the early 90s, during one of the worst droughts recorded in history, a friend of mine (a Native American), living in one of the pueblos, called me and asked, 'Gregg, would you like to join me for a prayer of rain?' He didn't have to ask twice; I said, 'You bet,' and I wasn't prepared for what I saw, because I expected I would see some chanting and some dancing, and what I saw was: where we met, at a prearranged place, my friend stepped to an ancient stone circle, he closed his eyes, turned his back to me, and about twenty seconds later he looked at me and he said, 'I'm hungry, you want to get a bite to eat?' And I said, 'Sure, but I thought you are going to pray for rain.' And this is where he looked at me. 'No,' he said, 'If I prayed for rain, rain could never happen, because the moment I ask for something to occur, I've just implied or agreed it's not there in this moment.' And I said, 'If you didn't pray for rain, what did you do just now?' And he said, 'When I closed my eyes I felt the feeling of what it feels like to stand with my naked feet in the mud of our pueblo village because there has been so much rain, and to smell the smells of the rain coming off the earth and the walls of our village, because there's been so much rain. And in that way I create the feeling of the rain.'"

Use mental rehearsal to breathe life into your vision. Create in your mind a few scenarios in which your wish has already come true. If you are looking for a relationship, see yourself having a romantic vacation with your partner, celebrating a birthday together, or introducing him or her to your family. If you are ill, picture yourself healthy and lively, having a good time with your loved ones and feeling wonderful. Once or a couple of times a day, focus on your desired vision until it becomes alive in your mind's eye and fills your heart with joy.

If you find it difficult to visualize, focus instead on filling yourself with the feelings you believe will accompany the fulfillment of your dream—serenity, satisfaction, happiness, freedom, ease, excitement, or any other feeling you wish for. The more these feelings become part of your life, the closer you get to realizing your dream.

When you find yourself thinking of a future event, notice whether you are assuming that your dream came true or that the current situation continues as it is. If your imagination pictures a future in which your dream has not come true, replace it with a new one in which your dream has already manifested.

Goal-supporting actions—In order to manifest what you want, your actions should be aligned with your wishes.

Avoid fear-driven actions, such as pleasing others, giving up what matters to you, and ignoring your feelings and needs, as well as actions that increase doubts, such as complaining about what you haven't achieved yet or about the fear that your dreams won't come true. Let go of blame toward your circumstances and the people that supposedly prevented you from achieving your goals.

Support the creation of what you want with actions that show your belief that your wish has already been answered, even if it hasn't yet materialized in physical reality; if, for example, you believe that when you have what you want, it will be easier for you to be patient with your parents, practice being patient with them now.

Often, when talking about manifestation, the following question comes up: "But what do I have to do to make my dream come true?" Since our perceptions of reality are responsible for the people and events we attract into our lives, an effective action won't involve a struggle. When your vision is alive and the desire to fulfill it is burning inside you, the right action reveals itself. As long as you are not clear about what you want or do not believe it is possible, your efforts will be futile.

Conscious dreaming—"If you can dream it, you can do it," said Walt Disney, explaining how it all started with one little mouse. In ways that are hard to explain, as my friend Seth says, "Life came from a dream."[7]

Conscious dreaming is a skill that should be practiced, the same as a muscle. It can support the creation of a wanted reality, help in solving the challenges we face, and strengthen self-confidence. It's also an invaluable tool for communication with those who are no longer in the physical body.

To strengthen your "dreaming muscle," try one of the following exercises. Make a wish before bedtime and then set it aside. Keep in mind that there might be a gap between the moment you make your wish and the time it appears in your dream, and if it doesn't work, simply try again.

- Ask to dream about a goal you wish to accomplish and to experience it as if it has already come true.
- When you are facing a challenge or struggling with an issue you are indecisive about, ask for support and direction in your dreams.
- If you are dealing with a health condition, ask for a dream in which the problem has already been solved and you are healthy.
- If a dream about a loved one that is not with you anymore raises guilt or pain, ask that the encounter in the dream will be loving and pleasant.

- Explore new ways of communication in your dreams—in the dream, take the initiative in a relationship in which you are usually passive, or try to express yourself assertively in situations where you tend to overreact.
- Use directive and healing dreams to process residues of pain and fear—One of my surprising experiences with dreaming is related to breaking free from my personal shell shock; when in the dream, the old scenario realized again in front of my eyes, I found myself reacting in a new way: instead of getting angry, I accepted the unwanted situation with calm. And at that moment, the old pain suddenly dissolved.

∴

Dare to dream; know that anything is possible; respect yourself and your wishes.

Afterword

The Principles Presented in This Book

1. The main keys to transforming your life are: A. You are creating your own reality. B. The moment of power is always the now.
2. All the problems you are facing come from deep-seated cultural thought patterns that create pain, fear, and lack of control. You are not damaged or broken. Anything can be changed.
3. The healing starts with letting go of blame toward your parents and anyone else you hold accountable for your life circumstances.
4. Only when you let go of what was "supposed" to be and what you "deserve" will you get what you really want.
5. The thinking mind cannot help you to effectively deal with the challenges you are facing; the solution lies within the dimension of presence—the portal to the infinite knowledge that is within and around you.
6. Every outcome has a reason; there is no coincidence or bad luck. Willingness to openly examine your inner state and actions, and attention to your thoughts, will teach you why whatever happens in your life happens.

7. Emotions are the key to the enormous power that is concealed within each of us.
8. Emotional drama, which can also be called negativity, is the destructive way in which human pain is perpetuated.
9. Love is the driving force of the universe.
10. You are 100% responsible for the show of your life, but you are not to blame for anything, as before you awaken you cannot control your creation.
11. The world always reflects what's inside you.
12. When you become present and can see what is in front of you, instead of the stories in your head, you can see that nothing is personal.
13. What most influences your feelings of worthlessness is deriving self-enhancement at the expense of others, selling yourself short for what you perceive as love, and constant self-judgment.
14. The key to happiness and success lies in the willingness to give up self-pity even before you have fulfilled your wishes.
15. When you quit doing what doesn't work, the right action reveals itself.
16. Without respect for yourself, others, the land, and all living things, nothing will be sustained over time.
17. You should trust yourself and your inner knowing. You need no advice.
18. Freedom is inherent in the essence of all living beings; you cannot give it up or deprive someone else of it without implications.
19. You can say anything as long as it comes from love. The words are not as important as the energy behind them.
20. The self has no limitations other than those you believe it has.

It Is All a Choice

In a course I attended, one of the participants told a story about her friend's daughter, who at the age of two, when she started talking, said to her mother, "There were many babies there, who didn't eat and talked through their heads, and I chose you." Her words touched a deep place within me, and confirmed what I already knew—we are the creators of our lives, nothing is coincidental, and we are never victims.

When I look at my life, at all the good moments as well as at the pain I've suffered, I'm amazed by the way things have developed, by the way the universe presented to me on a silver platter the opportunity to learn everything I needed to know, and it's clear to me that these experiences didn't happen by coincidence.

I'm excited for you when I'm thinking of the moment you will realize that no matter how old you are, whatever your gender or your race is, or what you have been through in your life, eventually you have chosen everything in order to get to this moment, to make a new choice, and to change the entire picture of your life.

A Glimpse into the Future

In the future, which is yet to come but I can already see it in my mind's eye, our emotions will guide us; there will be no need for authorities, rules, and law enforcement.

The well-being of children will be the top priority, and decency will be a cornerstone.

Committed relationships will be based on free will.

Freedom will be an innate right. No one will hold on to another or exploit him or her for personal needs.

The focus of education will be the development of essential life skills. Children will no longer attend school for years only to memorize and forget.

The oneness of mankind, beyond skin color, religion, race, or gender, will be clear to everyone.

Respect for the land and for all living things will be the norm, and we will all be aware of our connection to them.

The food will be natural and pure, and so will the air.

People will trust the ability of the body to heal itself; they will assume health, not sickness.

Elders will not be left alone.

And no one will die in fear, as everyone will know they are simply leaving the body to move on to another dimension of existence.

Conclusion

I urge you to get away from the screens, give up the news, feel the life around you, and be present with the ones you love, as there is no other time.

A Guide to Practicing Presence

In this guide you will find tools and directions that will help you implement the insights presented in this book in your daily life.

Basic Tools for Presence Practice

The basic tools may be integrated into your daily routine, for a second or a few seconds, as many times as possible during the day. Such a simple practice can create a significant change in your life.

The Five Senses

Using the five senses is the easiest way to enter the present moment:

- When you are walking down the street, instead of being immersed in thoughts, pay attention from time to time to what's around you—a tree, a flower, a balcony you have never noticed before, a bird flying, or the skyline.
- While sitting at home or at the office, from time to time look around without judgment.

- Listen to the sounds around you—a bird singing, a car passing by, the sound of an air conditioner, or a conversation in the distance.
- Feel a cool breeze coming through the window.
- Touch something, no matter what, and feel its texture.
- Smell the air after the rain or a fragrant flower.
- In the morning, before you get out of bed, pay attention to the position of your body on the mattress.

Conscious Breathing

- When you wake up, before your thinking has fully awakened, turn your attention to your breath—feel its natural rhythm and the ease with which it happens.
- During the day pause for a moment and give your fullest attention to one breathing cycle—from the beginning to the end.
- At night, when disturbing thoughts won't let go, focus your attention on your breathing. And if thoughts pop into your mind again, gently shift your attention back to your breathing.

Deepening Presence Through Daily Activities

No matter what you are doing right now—whether it's household tasks, duties at work, playing with the children, or anything else—turning your fullest attention to whatever you are doing provides relief from the burden of your thoughts. Instead of complaining about what you have to do, use any activity as a ticket into the present moment.

Creating Inner Peace from the Outside In

Screen activities take a large part of our time. They are highly addictive, increase restlessness and unhappiness, affect our relationships, and decrease attention span. In order to break free from screen dependency and create inner peace, try the following exercises:

- For one day or more, visit the social networks in which you are active only once a day. Examine how addicted you are to this habit, and notice the influence of avoiding it on your inner state.
- For a week, listen to a news update or look through one of the news portals no more than once a day. Avoid watching newscasts and current affairs programs. Examine the influence it has on your stress levels.
- When you are waiting somewhere or spending time with family or friends, instead of occupying yourself with the screen in front of you, look around and try to feel the life around you.
- Get an interesting new book and spend some time reading.
- If you are often falling asleep with the television on, try to avoid it, and take a few quiet moments before you go to bed.

Many people believe that the road is the perfect place to vent their anger. This so-called venting, however, doesn't relieve anything, it only intensifies their anger and negativity.

- If you are impatient and reactive on the road, pay attention to the impact of your reactions on your physical and emotional state. Next time, try to remain still and examine how it makes you feel.

Being Present with Another Person

Being present with another person adds another dimension, sometimes challenging, to presence practice. Since our lives are based on relationships, this is an essential skill.

Listening

Usually, even when we are quiet and the person in front of us is talking, the voice in our head is talking as well, interpreting what the other person is saying, thinking about other stuff, or looking for the right moment to interrupt him or her so we can talk about ourselves or give advice.

True listening, to differentiate, is the transfer of our full attention from the thoughts in our head to the other person's words and being fully present with him or her. When we listen in such a way, we allow ourselves a break from thinking about our problems and contribute to the relationship in a simple yet profound way.

Assumptions

We often assume that we know what those around us are thinking or feeling, based on what we thought or felt in similar cases. We make assumptions and act as if they were a fact. But while assumptions may sometimes be true, they are often mistaken.

Practice:
- Notice when you are making up negative scenarios in your head, and check the facts before you react.
- Always doubt your assumptions, even if you are sure you are right.

- Instead of making assumptions, look around, examine the state of mind of the other person, look for what's reflecting through his or her eyes, and read between the lines to understand the true meaning of his or her words.

Presence in the Face of Another Person's Emotional Turmoil

In times of crisis, false encouragement, such as, "He's not worth your tears," or, "He lost a deal of a lifetime," is not really helpful, as both the motivator and the listener know that the pretty words do not reflect the truth.

Instead, you can simply be present with the other person while accepting his or her feelings, without trying to rescue him or her.

Presence with Children

If you check what part of the time that you spend with your children you are really with them, you might discover that it's not much. What a child needs more than anything is for the parent to be present with him or her, without expectations, without trying to achieve something, without constant judgment or attempts to please him or her. If spending time this way becomes a habit, both you and the child will benefit from it tremendously.

Practice:

- When you sit next to your child, feel the warmth of his or her body and notice the rhythm of his or her breathing.
- When you walk hand in hand, pay attention to the feeling of your child's hand in yours.

- Look at his or her face or listen to his or her voice and cherish the uniqueness of the moment.
- When you are tempted to check your phone again, ask yourself if you can give it up and stay present with your child.

Self-Consciousness

Self-consciousness is the ability to look at ourselves, our actions, thoughts, and emotions without judgment, as if we were another person looking at us from the sidelines. When we develop the ability to look at ourselves this way, a gap between us and our thoughts is created, our identification with them subsides, and so does the pain they create.

It's also the willingness to acknowledge our true motives and our impact on others. Although doing so requires letting go of blame and taking full responsibility for our circumstances, it's the most powerful key to transforming ourselves and any relationship we are involved in.

Practice:

- A few times a day turn your attention to your thoughts and notice what you are thinking about. Don't judge the content of your thoughts and don't try to avoid thoughts that are perceived as negative.
- Ask yourself, "What is the message I'm sending to the other person, even if only beneath the surface?" and, "Is my energy appealing or repelling?"
- Examine the body sensations created by your words and actions. Notice an inner contraction, a burst of anger or pain, or alternatively, a feeling of comfort and inner peace.
- Listen to your thoughts, and every time you find yourself

dwelling on the past or creating frightening scenarios about the future, bring your attention back to the present moment and focus on what's around you. Don't worry if the exercise doesn't stop the negative thoughts, and notice how by recognizing the thought pattern, a gap, even if small, is created between you and your thoughts.

- Listen to your words and notice if you are speaking in the past or the future tense. Notice if your words conceal assumptions such as, "Everything could have been different," or, "This is what's going to happen." If so, try to use a neutral language that reflects the facts and examine the impact it has on your feelings.
- Notice whether the problem you are dealing with requires action at the present moment, or whether you are conducting an idle discussion about something that may or may not happen in the future.
- When you find yourself restless, check if you lost presence while exhausting yourself with the attempt to solve your problems by using rationalization, forcing positive thinking, or creating pros and cons lists in your mind.
- Associations game—Follow your thoughts and try to figure out how you came to think of a particular subject. "I was thinking of… which reminded me of… and then I came to think of…."

At first, self-consciousness might require energy and attention, but if you keep up with it, it will soon become second nature.

Breaking Free from Emotional Pain

The main thing that will help you break free from emotional pain is giving up emotional drama, as described in detail in chapter 6. Here I present you with some directions that will help you cope with emotionally charged situations.

- When you feel that more than anything you want to run away and can no longer stand the pain, keep communicating with the person you are talking to. Avoid hanging up the phone, running out the door, or withdrawing into yourself. When we don't obey the urge to run away, suddenly the picture clears up and the pain dissolves.
- If you avoid certain situations as you fear negative feedback or are afraid to face the subject of your jealousy, ask yourself, "Does avoiding these situations increase or decrease my fear?" "Does it make me feel calm or agitated?"
- Check whether judging yourself for unwanted feelings helps you release them, and see what happens when you acknowledge their unpleasant existence without self-judgment.
- Use presence to look through your pain-colored glasses, through the old illusion that automatically claims, "No one loves me," or, "No one wants my company." Stay still for a moment before you react and try to examine the facts.
- Notice statements that imply self-pity and resistance to *what is*, such as, "Why did it have to happen?" "I can't accept that," "I should be further along in life by now," "I feel like I'm only moving backward," "I can't stand it anymore," "I'm stuck," "It's not fair," or, "It can't be true

that she feels this way," and notice the impact of such statements on your feelings.

Breaking Free from Your Feelings of Worthlessness

Many techniques we use to feel better about ourselves actually deepen our sense of worthlessness. Thus, instead of working hard to improve our self-esteem, we can simply stop sabotaging it. Let's see how.

- During a day or a couple of days, notice every time you are judging yourself or talking to or about yourself with disrespect, and simply point it out to yourself: "I'm judging myself again," without being judgmental toward the fact that you are judging yourself.
- Do the same with self-pity, complaint, and blame. "I'm feeling sorry for myself," "I'm complaining," or, "I'm blaming him/her/them."
- Try to determine the purpose of your words. Are you trying to demean the other person or to emphasize your superiority? Do you feel the need to have the last word? Or maybe you are trying to force him or her to act in a certain way? If so, what feelings are associated with your actions?
- Be aware of the facial expressions and bodily gestures you are adding to your words, and ask yourself, "What am I trying to emphasize through these?"
- During a limited-time event, such as a lunch break, a social encounter, or a Pilates class, notice each time you are judging those around you, even if only in your head.

- When you avoid telling the truth about yourself (age, marital status, living conditions, occupation, etc.) examine the impact it has on your feelings. Try to speak the truth at a certain occasion without being apologetic and notice how you feel.
- If your sense of worth depends on positive reinforcement, try not to ask for it for a couple of days and notice the impact on your inner state.
- When you ask for advice, whether from a friend or from a professional, notice whether the conversation made you feel better or intensified self-criticism and confusion.
- If you are the one giving advice, examine if the advisor's role provides you with a sense of superiority. If so, just acknowledge your motives.
- From time to time ask yourself, "What do I think about this subject?" "What do I want?" and, "What do I feel?" without judging the answers that come up.
- Examine the measure of satisfaction you derive from a new accessory. For how long does it fill the emptiness within you? Does it make you feel worthy?
- Try not to follow the urge to justify yourself and protect your reputation, and see how it affects your sense of worth.
- If you are involved in an unhealthy relationship, ask yourself, "Is the value I'm getting worth the price I'm paying?"

∴

To best implement the exercises offered in this guide, as well as the insights offered in this book, choose one or more exercises to focus on for a day or a couple of days. Be compassionate with yourself—picture yourself as a baby who is taking his first steps; from time to time he falls, but once he recovers he (or she) gets up and keeps practicing the new skill.

Author Note

If you enjoyed this book, please think about leaving a review on Amazon, Goodreads, or any other platform of your choice. Your review will help other readers learn about the book and understand what makes it worth reading.

And if you wish to expand your understanding of the insights presented in this book, you are welcome to visit my website, where you will find the free guide "7 Simple Steps to Real Self-Love", interesting articles, and more.

Yours,
Sharon

www.sharonshahaf.com

References

1. The Factory Productions, Branding Illness, a film by Anne Georget and Mikkel Borch-Jacobsen, France, 2011.
2. American Psychiatric Association: Diagnostic and Statistical Manual of Mental Disorders. Fifth Edition. Arlington, VA: American Psychiatric Association, 2013.
3. Sittenfeld, Curtis. Prep. United States: Random House, Inc., 2005, Kindle Edition.
4. Roberts, Jane. The Nature of the Psyche: Its Human Expression (A Seth Book). San Rafael, CA. Amber-Allen Publishing, 1979, page 215.
5. Shani, Ayelet. "Ayelet Is Holding on to Grouchiness." Laisha Magazine (Israel), issue 3296, June 14, 2010. (Translated from Hebrew by Sharon Shahaf).
6. Braden, Gregg. Bathing In the Intelligent Force of the Universe. Host: Michael Toms. Interview Date: December 28, 2006.
7. Roberts, Jane. The Nature of the Psyche: Its Human Expression (A Seth Book). San Rafael, CA. Amber-Allen Publishing, 1979, page 222.

www.ingramcontent.com/pod-product-compliance
Lightning Source LLC
LaVergne TN
LVHW010313070526
838199LV00065B/5551